Science Fiction

Earth and Mars

...Finally the twins spin in harmony

R.K Murthi has been active in the field of writing for over four decades and has contributed over 4,000 articles, skits and profiles to leading English publications.

Author of more than 75 books, including biographies and stories and information books for children, (Many of them translated into other Indian languages), he received the NCERT Award for Children's Books in 1985 and again in 1997. In 1999, the Indo-Soviet Cultural Society honoured him for his lifetime contribution to the field of Literature for the Young. A former member of the Advisory Panel of the Nehru Bal Pustakalaya of the National Book Trust and a former head of the publication wing of the Children's Book Trust, he is currently the Secretary-General of the Indian Society of Authors.

Science Fiction

Earth and Mars

...Finally the twins spin in harmony

By

R.K. Murthi

Illustrations

Sonal Goyal

Sumit Sakhuja

UNICORN BOOKS

Publisher
UNICORN BOOKS

F-2/16, Ansari Road, Daryaganj, New Delhi-110002
☎ 011-23275434, 23262683, 23250704 • *Fax:* 011-23257790
E-mail: info@unicornbooks.in • *Website:* www.unicornbooks.in

Branch : Mumbai

23-25, Zaoba Wadi, Thakurdwar, Mumbai-401002

☎ 022-22010941, 022-22053387

E-mail: rapidex@bom5.vsnl.net.in

Showroom :

★ **PM Publications,** New Delhi

- 10-B, Netaji Subhash Marg, Daryaganj
New Delhi-110002
- 6686, Khari Baoli, Delhi-110006

ISBN 978-81-7806-106-1

Earth & Mars

Edition: 2012

Printed at: *Unique Color Carton, New Delhi-*

Dedication

To Uma and Mandeep

Contents

Author's Note *9*

Mission to Mars 13

The Rover Lands 55

The Swing of Spirits 93

Spin in Harmony 135

References *183*

Author's Note

This is a novel for children, in the older age group, who know of the vast expanse of the Universe that stretches unto infinity and of recent successes in space exploration. It comes under the genre of science fiction.

How did I get the idea for this novel? I don't know. A psychologist may explain the mystery. All that I know for certain, being familiar with science to some extent, is that the reports I watched over the TV charged a few of my brain cells and made them hyperactive. The buzz led to a few nerve cells getting connected, in a new pattern, and ideas started flowing through these links with a spurt of creativity. This linking happened, if I may admit, purely by chance.

This happened on January 5, 2004, while I was watching the TV news. The anchorperson spoke of the landing of Rover Spirit, an American space machine, on Mars. The report also stated that another machine, named Rover Opportunity, was closing in on Mars and would be landing, half way across Mars, away from the site of landing of Rover Spirit, in three week's time. The main thrust of the Mars Mission, said the reports, was to confirm the presence of water and also to track down life forms, if any, on Mars.

The report made me sit up. Myriad ideas filled my head. These ideas related to a variety of scientific facts I had gathered since the time the first spaceship, a satellite of the Earth, was placed in orbit by the Soviet Union. The Soviet Union maintained its lead when Yuri Gagarin became the first astronaut. Then began a race for space probes. America snatched the lead in 1969 when man first touched down on the Moon. Since then, there have been efforts to pry into the planets of the Solar System and also of the Galaxies, some of them millions of

Light Years away, by all developed nations of the world.

Mars is one of the Planets closest to the Earth. (The other is Venus). Many scientists refer to Mars as the Earth's Twin. The landing of the Rovers on Mars provided me a chance to produce a science fiction in which I could use the freedom of the creative writer while sticking to scientific facts. This blend of fact and fiction, if effective, makes a lasting impact on the target audience. The reader absorbs several scientific concepts while he goes through the novel. The knowledge he acquires stays firmly embedded in his mind. That justifies this fictional work.

I present the novel to the readers, with the hope that the storyline, deftly woven round facts, fetches them double rewards, namely entertainment and learning.

New Delhi

—R.K. Murthi

1

Mission to Mars

Pasadena is in a remote area of California. Here, one of the major centres of NASA, the prime space research organization of the United States, is located. Spread over a vast area, tightly secured by high walls and massive steel gates and sensitive equipment, including electronic eyes and warning systems, to prevent unauthorised entry into the premises, it remains impregnable.

The identity of everyone who works at the complex is established by matching the employee's fingerprints with those stored in the central computer. More recently, so run unconfirmed reports, efforts are on to have a sort of biological profile in which the employee's DNA, drawn from the sweat glands, is tested against the available records in the central computer.

The complex is further secured against aerial snooping by a series of radars and also jamming equipment that make it virtually impossible to see what is happening within the complex.

On Sunday, January 4, 2004, Dr. Wilson Cockroff, the Chief of the Mars Mission Centre, at Pasadena, sat at the oval-shaped glass-topped table in his spacious office, his eyes fixed on a large computer screen that showed the Mars Rover Spirit streak closer to the Planet Mars.

He was short and stout, with a grizzly growth all around his cheeks and chin. One wondered whether a wren could comfortably have built a nest in his flowing beard. His eyes had a steely glint that indicated how focused and determined he was.

He was a teenager when he first read about satellites. The Russians had taken the lead by placing the Sputnik in space and later sending Yuri Gagarin in an orbit round the earth, gaining for him eternal fame as the first astronaut. While the Russian achievement excited him, Dr. Cockroff still felt a slight unease. He was an American and be had been told again and again that, of all the nations in the world, America was the first and the best in every way. The Soviets had given a body blow to the pre-eminence of the United States, felt the boy, by stealing the honours in space research. Why did America lose the race? Possibly, he argued, young men with the necessary scientific skill were not entering the field.

That marked the moment of decision for Wilson Cockroff. He resolved that he would study Physics, enter the space research programme and do his bit to redeem the nation's pride.

Physics had always been his pet subject at school where he was a contemporary of George Bush Jr., now the President of the United States. They were fairly close in those days, close enough to address each other, not by the first name, but by the last name, suitably amended to make them exclusive. George called Cockroff, COCKY; and the latter found the right reference to the rich playboy that George was in the word BUSHY.

Both parted ways, after completing their education. They drifted apart and but for New Year greetings there was hardly any contact between the two. Not till George Bush became Governor and went round to visit some of the Space Stations and renewed contact with Cocky, then heading a division, planning the Mission to Mars. Since then, they had been in touch, though both had their careers to chase. George Bush had set his goal on the Presidency, resolved that he would leave no stone unturned to enter the White House that had once housed his father. Dr. Cockroff had his eyes on the planets of the Solar System and the stars and the galaxies beyond. Both had their goals; and both were totally focused.

After completing his master's degree in high efficiency propulsions, Cockroff chose to study refinements in the design of the projectiles to make the take off smoother and more efficient. He also briefed himself on special fuels that would give more thrust to the launching of rocket systems for his doctoral work.

In January 1979, he joined NASA. Six months later, he was at a party to celebrate the 10th anniversary of man's landing on the moon. He heard the seniors at the Centre recollecting the scene of that triumph when Neil Armstrong and Edwin Aldrin had set foot on lunar soil. They had behaved, they said, like school children on a wild spree on the night the school closed for a long vacation, shouting and screaming and singing, hugging and smooching and lifting and rolling with anyone within reach, giving full expression to the joy at the success of the lunar mission. They asserted that they could never capture that excitement in word pictures. "Not till we land a man on Mars will we feel equally thrilled," the head of the group dropped a dream that he knew could take a long long time to come true. But, dream he did. That dream became the dream of everyone there, including Dr. Wilson Cockroff.

In those days he was a compact, short yet well-proportioned young man of 30, an eager beaver, intent on proving to his seniors that he had it in him to occupy higher positions of responsibility.

His rise was rapid, but it cost him much in terms of personal life. He began to spend more and more time at work.

That left him with very little time to continue his date with his girlfriend, Sandra

Markosheva, whose great grandparents had migrated from Poland and landed, in 1903, after a hard rocky passage in a small ship that weathered the vagaries of the Atlantic crossing, at Ellis Island, across New York, then the entry point of immigrants, penniless, yet confident of finding a future for themselves in the land of immense opportunities. For nearly two years, she pleaded with him to find a fine balance between work and personal life. He promised to do her bidding, but every promise ended up as yet another pledge, thrown to the wind, not because he wanted to play false to her, but because he often got totally engaged in work and thus lost track of time and failed to keep his appointment with her.

Sandra realized, soon, that he loved her, but he loved his work more than he loved her. She was not willing to play second fiddle to his first love. She would have him on her terms or she would turn her back to him. She held out that ultimatum. Dr Cockroff stared at her, shocked out of his wits, hoping against hope that she would agree to be his wife and also learn to be tolerant of his fierce dedication to science. She firmly turned down his plea. She wished him well, smiled wryly, shook hands with him and turned off, tears in her eyes and choked sobs in her throat. Never again did she cross his path. Nor had he time to track her down. She became a back number in his life.

In the beginning, it was a little hard to accept the reality. He thought Sandra, if she truly loved him, should have been willing to accept him for what he was. It took some time for him to realise that she could hurl the same argument at him, ask him why he wanted to give science more importance in his life than his wife.

The truth then struck him. He was a crank, totally unsuited to the life of a happy married man. No woman would ever be happy with him. Not with his near-total commitment to scientific research. Once that insight put in roots, he found it easy to forget Sandra. He thanked Sandra for driving him into the arms of his one love, Science. He considered himself lucky because he found all the pleasure he sought in chasing crazy ideas in the field of planet studies. He told himself that he was better off remaining a bachelor, joked to his mother who raised the issue of marriage a few times, "Mamma, I am not a bachelor, as you assume. You ought to know that I am wedded to my work." She thought that rather stupid and angrily asserted that he would miss the warmth of the home, of a tender wife and a bunch of loving children, in his old age. "But Mamma, I may never grow old. Genetics is the latest branch of science. Once we conquer genes, we beat old age too," he said. His mother turned away, growling, "You are a silly old fool" while he laughed and added, "A silly old fool deserves no wife."

Better a silly old fool in the eyes of his mother than a silly old fool in the eyes of the whole world! Oh! How he wished he could satisfy her. He did his best, but he refused to marry.

Now that marriage prospects receded, he could devote himself totally to his work. He spent all the waking hours at the laboratory; found very little time for physical exercises, bloated up like a balloon. His peers recognized him as a rising star in the field and assigned him more responsibilities. That put a pressure on his time. He thought about it. Then he saw a way out. He could save time by not brushing his hair as often as he used, by keeping the razor away from the chin and letting a beard cover up his cheeks and chin. He did that. He ended up with thick unruly hair and a luxurious though unkempt beard.

The Lunar probe was only the first step in man's conquest of space. Success always acts like heady wine. The success of the lunar missions breathed more confidence into the army of scientists who worked for NASA. The organization felt ready to travel beyond the Moon, a satellite of the Earth, to the Planets of the solar system and also to the vast wide space beyond the Solar System. Dr. Cockroff played a major role in the subsequent space probes.

It was at the party held to celebrate the landing of man on the Moon, as we already noted, that Dr. Cockroff first heard the dream plan to probe Mars and, if possible, to land a man on Mars. He knew, immediately that he would hitch his stars to the Mars bandwagon. For that he had first to find entry into the small group that was being gathered around to take on the project. He did not let the grass grow under his feet. He waited for the right time to seek the help of his section head, Col. Marsh Goven.

He got the chance soon enough. After discussing a new idea for a better fuel-efficient propellant design, Dr. Cockroff casually enquired whether the members of the team to work on Mars had already been identified. The Colonel fixed him with a stern stare and then burst into laughter. "I thought you were moonstruck."

"I am not that mad, Colonel," Dr. Cockroff replied, almost instantly, noting that the term moonstruck carried distinct hints of mental imbalance.

"You are either mad or you are a genius," Col. Marsh Goven quipped, before leaning forward, enquiring with a tone of mild amusement whether he was serious of getting Mars-struck.

"Yes, Colonel. Better be Mars-struck than be moonstruck. At least, people will say that I reached for a much bigger target than a mere satellite of the Earth," Dr. Cockroff made his reason clear.

"I thought you cared not for people and not for how they viewed you," Col. Marsh Goven leaned back and sent his chair rotating at a fairly fast pace.

"I do, Colonel. I do. I care for people with a mission in life."

"And you think Mars is your mission?"

"You got it right, Sir. If you think I fill the bill, please recommend my name for possible inclusion in the team that will work on the Mission to Mars," Dr. Cockroff's voice was one of pleading.

"Have I ever I failed you, my boy?" Col. Marsh Goven exploded, in mock anger, before bursting into laughter, "Do you know that I have already sent your name to the Chief?"

"Thank you, Colonel, I can never thank you adequately," Dr. Cockroff had tears in his eyes, tears that reflected the joy at his senior's initiative and the feelings of gratitude that filled his heart.

"You damn young fool!" the Colonel rose from his seat, came round, held Dr. Cockroff's hand and pressed it warmly.

That was one scene that Dr. Cockroff never forgot.

Within a month, he was inducted into the team formed to develop suitable plans for a Mars probe.

The first meeting of the team, soon after its formation, was held under the chairmanship of Brigadier Mrs. Verita Bugeron. The 45 year-Army veteran was a well-proportioned woman, endowed with a figure and matching looks that belied her age. She had a buccolic sense of humour, but did not have immense technical expertise. What gave her the right to head the group was her extraordinary ability to coordinate and get the best out of those who worked with her. She was known to be a no-nonsense woman who would not hesitate to walk into the chamber of the most irate boss and beg, plead, argue, quote rules and regulations of which she was a past master, refuse to give up till her suggestions and recommendations were accepted. Dr. Cockroff found her tenacity infectious. Quite a few of her colleagues and juniors found the right adjective to describe her. They said she was single-minded. When she heard the term tagged on to her, she said, while rocking with laughter, "I have only one mind. Thank God! That makes it easy for me to make up my mind. Those with too many minds shall always be indecisive, always dither in moments of crisis."

Dr. Cockroff found that logic invincible. He learnt from her the advantage of having a cool head and a level thinking. He observed her, in action, took the necessary cues, and became a clone of her as far as decisiveness was concerned. She, in turn, found in him a potential leader of men and took him under her wings.

She left after a couple of years, to rejoin the Forces, but she ensured that her protégé would have the right career progress. He rose, by dint of hard work, matched by immense depth of understanding of the field of projectiles, to positions of responsibility.

The first probes of the Mars had begun in the 1960s. Dr Cockroff joined only in 1980, but he made up for lost time by reading all available material on the Planet. He became so familiar with the background that he could, even in his sleep, roll out amusing facts about the Planet.

Why did the Romans name it the God of War? They noticed the blood red colour of Mars, instantly remembered the bloody battlefields at which they had shown their valour and courage and taken a heavy toll of the enemy forces and found it right to hail Mars as the God of War. The Babylonians accepted Mars as Nergal, the God of Death and Pestilence. The Greeks called it Ares or the God of Battle, claimed that the Planet's two satellites, Phobos (Fear) and Deimos (Terror), were the sons of Ares and Aphrodite.

He could give every detail about the Planet . . . its distance from the sun; its diameter, its tilt to the axis, (imaginary though it be), the time it takes for one revolution round the axis, the time it takes to go round the sun once, the once held belief of a network of canals on its surface. He could also list all the famous astronomers whose work collectively took man closer to a better understanding of the Planet.

His mastery over the technical details relating to the probe of Mars was absolute. One could safely assert that his knowledge of the Planet was not a wee little bit inferior to what the best of encyclopedias provided. He would go into ecstasy, while pointing out that observations of Mars are best made 'when the planet is in the opposite direction in the sky to the Sun (i.e., opposition), allowing all-night viewing when Mars is closest to the Earth. Successive oppositions occur at intervals of approximately 26 months. Oppositions occur at different points in the Martian orbit; those that occur near perihelion are best, because the planet is then closest to both the Earth and the Sun and, therefore, is bright and large. The orbital plane of Mars is inclined at an angle of 1.85° to the Earth's orbital plane. At Martian perihelion, Mars is well south of the Earth's orbital plane. So, during favourable oppositions Mars is best observed from sites south of the Equator.'

Slipped under the glass top of the table one found a neat computer print out that gave brief details of Mars.

Average diameter—4,200 miles (6,720 km)

Average distance from the Sun—141,600,000 miles (226,600,000 km)

Average speed in orbit—54,200mph/86,700 kmph).

Time to make one orbit—687 Earth Days.

Time to spin once around itself—24.5 Earth Hours.

Temperature in Summer at the Equator

Day—21 degree Centigrade.

Night—80 degree Centigrade.

Number of Moons—Two. Phobos and Deimos.

His eyes would gain sparkles when he dwelt at length on the dark markings that cover about one-third of the total area of the Martian surface, of the remaining terrain with subtle shadings and intricate features and also of the so-called Martian canals about which much was said by Percival Lovell, one of the greatest astronomers of the 19th century.

Even obscure facts about Mars were not unknown to Dr Cockroff.

His colleagues saw how passionately devoted he was to Mars and started referring to him as Dr. Martian. He did not mind this gentle dig. He found no cause for annoyance in the nickname. On the contrary, he found it quite amusing to be called by that name and often used the term himself, with a merry twinkle in his eyes, adding, "How I wish that would come true! Then I will be able to know all about Mars. The Planet shall then hold no secret from me."

By mid 2002, he became the Chief of the Mars Mission Team that planned to land two spacecrafts on Mars and to equip them with the technology to roam around the Planet. Mars Rovers *Spirit* and *Discovery* became his pet babies. He took an active part in the design and also in deciding on the equipment that the Rovers would have on board to carry out the probe of Mars's surface. Placing the Rovers in space and setting them on a path that would take them to Mars was perhaps the easiest part of the whole project. The danger lay in equipping the Rovers to cut through the thin atmosphere of Mars. Even if Rovers landed safely, there still remained the rather complex issue of providing the Rover with suitable means of moving over the dusty soil. Dr. Cockroff held long discussions with automation engineers, debated several options, discarded quite a few before finally approving the design of hopping motion for the Rovers that looked akin to the leaps of frogs. Asked why he chose this mode of movement, he explained, a smile touching his lips, "Ever plodded through layers of sand? Is it not better to move with hops, steps and jumps over such terrain?" and added, as if it was an afterthought, "As the frog moves."

The usual equipment of radar controls and sophisticated cameras on board the Rovers were further augmented by one additional capability, something that was the result of a brainwave that Dr. Cockroff had. On previous occasions, the Mars probes were limited to search for bacteria, as we know them on the Earth. Dr. Cockroff wondered whether that was justified. Suppose that life forms on Mars had evolved from a differently structured bacterial base! Then search for life by adopting conventional manmade tests would fail.

The more he thought of it, the more did he become convinced of the need to follow this idea to the very end. It could end up as a wild goose chase. But that was a risk he was willing to undertake. "Nothing dared, nothing achieved," he mumbled to himself while he picked up the intercom and asked Dr. Pantulu Paramsiva Sastri, a scientist who headed the genetic division of the Central Lab, acknowledged as the best genetic engineer at the establishment, whether he could drop in at his office for a chat.

Dr. Sastri, born at a village close to Tenali in Andhra Pradesh in India, had arrived in the United States as a young dreamy-eyed biologist to pursue higher studies at one of the prestigious universities in the United States. He had worked with Dr. Har Gobind Khurana, the famous scientist, who too was of Indian origin and had migrated to the United States, worked in the field of genetics, emerged as a leading light in the field and won the Nobel Prize.

Dr. Sastri was tall and slim, with a light brown skin and a nose that bore unmistakable similarity to the beak of an eagle. Some of his admirers made fun of his nose, joked that he could poke his nose into even the most inhospitable of Planets and even if it got caught in a wedge he could pull it out unscathed by exploiting the rule of lever power that gives advantage to the long handle.

"Cocky, how are you, old boy?" Sastri, who was on first name basis with the Chief of the Mission, walked in, and shook hands with the senior vigorously.

"Param, Can you sniff out a method by which we could test a possible theory?" Dr. Cockroff didn't even wait to offer Dr. Sastri a chair.

"Cocky, at times your are too cocky, so cocky that you end up as a poor host? I think I will have to find a seat on my own. If I wait for your invitation, I may be left standing till eternity," Dr. Sastri sank into the cushioned seat, from where he could have eyeball-to-eyeball contact with his senior.

"Sorry, Param. I am Dr. Martian and no Martian ever feels the need to be polite," Dr. Cockroff laughed.

"I should have remembered," Dr. Sastri rocked with laughter and his nose swung like a pendulum slowing down, making very small arcs in space.

NASA
NASA

"Now, tell me, Param, on this earth, life chain has carbon at the base. Suppose it is not so on Mars?" Dr. Cockroff bent forward, his chest touching the rim of the glass-topped table, his fingers starting to drum the table.

"Who can say for sure? Only Lord Venkatachalapati . . ."

"Who is He? Is he an Indian scientist whom the Queen of England honoured with a knighthood? Get hold of him. Ask him if he knows about the base of life on Mars?" Dr. Cockroff broke in, his voice quivering with excitement, while his hand gently caressed his thick beard.

"I am talking of God! Lord Venkatachalpathi is my family deity, the God who protects me, the God to whom I pray daily. You may look upon the Lord as my Guardian Angel."

"Oosh," Dr. Cockroff's hopes crumbled like a balloon that had been suddenly pricked by a needle. "I thought you were dropping the name of another Indian with a scientific bent of mind."

"You got it wrong, Cocky."

"Not my fault, Param. Every Indian seems to me a scientist. Look at the present Mission to Mars that we are planning. Kanna Rajan is developing MAGPEN, (Mixed Initiative Activity Planning Generator), the software for the ground based decision support system needed to guide the Rovers while giving them maximum autonomy. They will be powered by low temperature lithium ion rechargeable batteries developed by Ratna Kumar Bagga. The lead Engineer who will oversee the landing is Prasun Desai. Other scientists of Indian origin include Mohana Gurrum, Vishwanath Magapu and Tarang Patel. I can roll on more names, though quite a few of them are tongue-twisters for me," Dr. Cockroff leaned back and tried a little rotation of his swinging chair.

"It isn't easy for us, either, Cocky, to take the name of quite a few Americans either. Your name is Cockroff, but you insist we make the last ROFF sound like ROUGH," Dr. Sastri grinned.

"You and your weird sense of humour!" Dr. Cockroff growled, in good humour, before assuming a serious note, "Can we incorporate in the Rovers some system that will tell us if there is life on Mars and if so what evolutionary track it followed to thrive in a setting that is totally inhospitable to us?"

"Theoretically, it is possible," Dr. Sastri's words revived the hope of Dr. Cockroff.

"Go on," Dr. Cockroff nudged.

"Well, I don't know whether it would work, but it is worth trying. Suppose we add to the panel on board the Rovers special sensors that exploit genetic technology and enable the Rovers to sense what even the cameras can't catch. Matching sensors at the ground station may also `see' what the sensors see. We could even provide a magic eye that could not only sense but see even the tiniest of life form, if detected, on Mars," Dr. Sastri took a deep breath.

Dr. Cockroff thought of it as a move in the right direction. If there were life forms on Mars, the special eye might sense them. Or it might not. There was nothing certain about the sensor leading the team closer to the solution of the riddle about life on Mars. Yet, it certainly was worth trying.

"Go ahead, Param. Your idea appeals to me. It needs to be chased to the very end," Dr. Cockroff sounded quite relieved while he gently freed a few strands of knotted hair of his luxurious beard.

"Which means you won't groan and grunt if we make demands for more finance allocation," Dr. Sastri wanted to be sure of the ground.

"I promise," Dr. Cockroff knew a good thing when he ran into it. "This is a matter of pride for the United States. The European Space Agency is out to beat us to the game.

That should not happen. Once the Soviets put us behind. They managed to put Sputnik in space. They beat us again in the race when Yuri Gagarin became the first man in space. Oh! How hard we fought to catch up with the Soviet Union!"

"You went beyond that. You broke up the Soviet Union itself," Dr. Sastri broke in.

"Leave politics out, Param."

"Because you know nothing about politics of power, played by Super Powers," Dr. Sastri added.

"Let us limit our debate to space probes," Dr. Cockroff fixed Param down with a firm glance. "We won the race to send man to the Moon and claimed the lead. Since then we are in the lead. Now the Europeans are trying to score over us. No. That shall not happen. So God help us."

"God helps those who help themselves," Dr. Sastri quietly hissed.

"Then we are going to help ourselves," Dr Sastri didn't miss the touch of finality in the tone of Dr Cockroff.

"Our orbiter Mars Odyssey is circling Mars for more than one year and filing significant information," Dr. Sastri rejoined.

"We now know that the Polar Caps of Mars contain frozen water," quietly Dr. Cockroff added.

"That indicates possibility of life form on Mars," Dr. Sastri peered expectantly at Dr. Cockroff.

"We are out to resolve the issue. The technology you suggested could be the key to the problem," Dr. Cockroff grinned.

"It could be," Dr. Sastri seemed still to have reservations about the whole design.

"Param. I am an incurable optimist," Dr. Cockroff stretched his hands above his head, trying to restore blood circulation through his limbs.

"I have never seen a curable optimist, all my life," Dr. Sastri rose from his seat, ready to get back to his lab, now that he knew what Dr. Cockroff expected of him.

"Bye, for the present," Dr. Cockroff reached out to shake hands with Dr. Sastri.

The sensor began as a blueprint, which underwent a thousand changes, at various stages of testing and verification, before the first prototype was made and subjected to rigorous screening. Again and again, the team saw their hopes end up in dismay when one flaw or the other popped up, unexpectedly. But, like Robert Bruce, the legendary King with a never say die spirit, the members of the team refused to give up. Each failure hardened the will of the team led by Dr. Sastri to continue the chase for the elusive design that would make the sensor operationally perfect. Their efforts led them, finally, to success. The final design of the sensor was tested and found to work with perfect accuracy. A special display meet was held at which a panel of experts grilled Dr. Cockroff and Dr Sastri on every area of doubt that the panelists had. Finally the idea was cleared. The sensors were installed on board the panel of the Rovers.

Dr. Sastri also worked on a Thought Reader, TR for short.

The idea for the TR came from his wife, Dr Sarah Beligner, a psychiatrist.

They had met, first, at a New Year party, about fifteen years back. She was then a curvaceous young woman, preparing for her MD in psychiatry. She won him over by telling him, "You are honest to the core, Param. I can see that in your body language."

"Has body a language?" he asked in all innocence.

"That is where we psychiatrists hold the edge. You need language to communicate. At the same time, you are sending several other signals. You raise your eyelids; or you turn your face away, avoiding a direct glance; or a frown sprouts on your forehead. There are a million signs, each one conveying a message to one who knows how to read them," she laughed, while coming a little closer to him.

"Have you to come so close to read the signs?" he joked.

"I wish I could get closer, but your nose stands in the way," she joked.

"It is my guardian angel," he bantered.

"Wonder how far it can be one, if and when a woman casts her spell on you and wriggles into your heart and claims you as her own," she smiled, revealing dimples that added to her beauty.

"Are you trying to do that? If my mother hears of it, she will be furious. She wants me to marry her brother's daughter," he sighed, feeling unsure of what was happening to him. An intense craving to take her in his arms coursed through him. He felt as if he could spend a lifetime with her. His face revealed the emotions. She did not miss it.

"Don't fall for me. My first love is my profession," she giggled.

"That is so with me too," he replied.

"In which case I could even add that we are made for each other," her smile seemed to stretch from ear to ear.

"Who knows for sure? This could be the will of Lord Venkatachalapati . . ." he cut short his words.

"Who is this Lord?"

"He is the Lord of Tirumalai. He is a God who is eternally in debt. He borrowed some money from Kubera, the God of wealth. And this debt, we are told, will never be cleared."

"Once you get into the grip of a money lender, there is no redemption. A loan from a shark is a one-way road to ruin. But can't the Lord . . . Venkat . . ." she struggled, shirked her shoulders, decided not to bother about getting the name right, and continued, "Can't the Lord say that he can't pay any longer because his nose has caved in under the strain of the continuous flow of money into the cash box of Kubera? Or has the Lord a nose as strong and as 'outgoing' as yours?" she burst into laughter.

A few more meetings later, the two decided to be man and wife. Both continued to date their first loves and hence found very little time to be together, yet they learnt to make the best of every moment they spent in each other's company. Their marriage was a perfect success. Each understood the other's commitment to the chosen field of work. All else came next. The only thing that did not come next was a child. But neither of them seemed to worry over that. Dr. Sastri thought it too was the Lord's will. "The Lord has no time for anything else but to clear His debt. So how can He find time to gift us a baby?" she perked up with a comment that made both of them rock with laughter.

She suggested to him, one day, when they got time for themselves, about the TR.

"Listen, dear! Suppose there are intelligent beings on Mars! How will you communicate with them?" she asked.

He stumbled for an answer. He threw up his hands and then scowled, "Hi, silly Billy, are you saying that you want to go to Mars to read the sign languages? If so, forget it. I shall not let you go."

"Who is talking of going to Mars? I still love life; and I would be the last one to go to a place where you have an atmosphere severely laden with Carbon dioxide," she paused before adding, "How about adding to the equipment on board the Rovers a machine that could, if it spots intelligent life forms, be able to fathom their thoughts?" she intertwined her fingers in his and looked into his eyes, waiting for his response.

"You live up to your pet name, Billy. You mew like a cat demanding a saucer of milk," he joked, before adding in a serious tone," That is the best of suggestions I have heard from you ever. I congratulate myself for leading you to the couch, you who lead your clients to the couch and make them cough out their innermost secrets. That makes me superior to you, a headshrinker," he merrily cracked a series of light remarks that made her giggle uncontrollably, for some time.

Later, they debated the suggestion. "Could it be possible to develop a TR?" he asked.

"That's your headache," she dodged.

"You are the cause of this headache. And I hate you for that," he feigned disgust.

"I read it as a sham hate," she rose to fetch him a cup of hot coffee.

Dr. Sastri consulted Dr. Cockroff, when they met next, about the suggestion.

"Why not?" Dr. Cockroff was enthusiastic.

Thus, when the two Rovers were readied, both the ideas of Dr. Sastri were incorporated. The Rovers had on board the Special Sensor and the Thought Reader. They were embedded in one module that came to be referred to as SSTR.

"Oh! If only we find life form on Mars!" Dr. Cockroff mailed his fists and swung it like a golfer, taking aim before the strike after watching the Rover Spirit take off in the last week of June 2003. He repeated the same wish when Rover Opportunity was launched in the first week of July 2003.

For six months, the Rovers moved through the wilderness of space, heading toward Mars. Ground control monitored their progress. Dr. Cockroff could not wait for the day of the landing. The wait seemed interminable. He swung between hope and despair during the long wait. He could never get over the mood of uncertainty. He knew that there could be many a slip between the cup and the lip. The Rovers might get close to Mars and descend, only to crash on the Planet. Or they could land but the communication system might get jammed and snap links with the ground station. These fears nagged him continuously. He learnt to live with fears saying, "Fear is the key."

He was lucky, however, in one way. His fears would have gained wings if he had known that Mars had sent spies to the Earth, that the spies remained invisible to man, while managing, despite the tight security around the Mission complex, to overhear bits and pieces of conversation of the scientists while they were outside the complex, at hotels or motels or restaurants, in cubicles exclusively reserved for them and where no outsider could intrude, to learn of the special sensor that had been mounted on the Rovers and alerted the top leadership of Mars. The spies could do that easily because their genes made them invisible to all but the Martians, and so not even the most alert security official could get wind of the clandestine activities of the Martian spies.

Thankfully, Dr. Cockroff too remained ignorant of the spy network of Mars on the Earth. So the only fear he had to contend with was the possibility of the failure of the Rovers. How much more scary would the scene have been if he had been told that his best-laid plans of a sensor to track down life on Mars had been passed on to the rulers of the Red Planet.

Sometimes ignorance can be bliss. It was so for Dr. Cockroff, on this occasion.

❑❑❑

2

The Rover Lands

Raja Marspati, the ruler of Planet Mars, did not get agitated easily. He remained cool and collected, believed that losing one's mental balance never did anyone any good. He had no doubts in his mind that in moments of crisis one who retained his head survived. Raja Marspati was keen to keep not only his head, but also the crown on his head; and that, he knew, demanded of him the courage to face every situation with a never-say-die spirit. Even when fear gripped him, he did not show the slightest trace of it on his face. He had mastered the art of bottling up his feelings within and projecting the image of a Martian, perfectly confident and in complete control over the situation, though deep within, all sorts of dangerous possibilities whirled around in his head, giving wings to his fears. Yet he had in the past, refused to buckle down to fears, managed to retain his regal mien. Rarely ever in his long regime of more than forty years had anyone seen him react in panic.

However, rarely ever as we all know, doesn't mean NEVER.

The report, sent by the agents on Planet Earth that the Earthlings had launched Rovers that carried highly developed technical equipment to track down life forms on Mars, had taken him by surprise. For a million years, the existence of life forms on Mars had been kept as a closely guarded secret from denizens of other Planets. The State of technological advancement of Mars was far ahead of that on the Earth and the Raja had assumed that this gap would never be bridged. But, in the last hundred years or so, the curiosity of the Earthlings had been insatiable. Reports, filed by agents of Mars on the Earth, in the first three quarters of the 20th Century, spoke of developments in rocketry and the landing of man on the Earth's Moon and the ongoing projects to study the other planets of the Solar System and also to probe the Milky Way. It was evident that the Earthlings were geared to move beyond the limits set by the Earth's gravity. They were now talking of colonizing the Planets and of exploiting the riches of the Planets. That approach of the Earthlings roused the Raja's fears.

He cursed himself and his forefathers for not taking to colonization a million years ago. He wondered whether he should, even at this late stage, use the Martian Ray that could turn the Earth into vapour in seconds. He held the power to use it, in an emergency. The Red button that would send the Ray streak through space was right within his reach. Yet he had held back the final step.

Was he justified in not nipping the problem in the bud? He was not quite sure, though he was eager, if possible, to make friends with the Earthlings. He had learnt, while he was the heir apparent and was trained by some of the best brains of the land, that the Earth and the Mars could be viewed as twins. For they shared several common features; chief among these features was their size. Moreover they were close to each other. They were neighbours. Good relation with the Earth, therefore, could prove beneficial to both the Planets.

But he still had his fears. For the Earthlings were going about, asserting that they were the finest creations of God, that they would soon colonise the Moon and Mars and the other Planets. In other words, the Earthlings were dreaming of conquests of the Planets. If only the Earthlings extended the hand of friendship to the Martians! If only!

But there was no sign of such an attitude on the part of the Earthlings.

Raja Marspati looked slightly agitated as he paced the carpeted veranda of his palace, often reaching out for one of the two slight bulges at the extremes of the head, in line with the top of the forehead, as if he was seeking some support to still the nagging fear within and to regain his usually unruffled posture. The action was involuntary, almost instinctive. It was as if the Raja found in the bulge the steadying force. These slight protuberances were not exactly horns, though the citizens of Mars did refer to them by that name. The horns were what made the race distinct. Every Martian had them.

Many were the legends associated with the horns.

All Martians claimed that they were splitting images of their God, Marseshwara, that the Lord had very strong and powerful horns. The idols of the Lord, installed in the

temples to Marseshwara, invariably displayed the horns prominently. Every sculptor lent to the horns the touch of power and glory, made them extra large, reaching up to the roof of the sanctum sanctorum and in some cases, where the artists felt that even the roofs should not set limits to the horns, showing them piercing the roof and moving up as far as possible toward the sky.

Some modern artists played with the Lord's form to produce highly original images. One artist gained fame by portraying Marseshwara in a dance posture; another emerged as a trend setter in the field by showing Him in a reclining pose; and a third one gained name and fame by depicting the Lord fighting a demon and pinning him down under His feet and goring him with His sharp horns. Artists and idol-makers tried out every possible form and shape to represent the God as one moving with the times. Many temples that came up during the regime of Marspati had idols of the Lord dressed up during occasions, in the latest of dresses, fashioned by the leading lights in the field.

Idol makers, who worked with clay, let their creativity scale great heights during the annual festival of the land, known throughout the Planet as *Marsehwaraleelotsav*, which fell during the summer months. For ten days, every Martian, but for few exceptions, took part in the festivities, held in every nook and corner of the vast land. The air around the Planet became charged with the spirit of the festive season. On the last day, the idols were ceremoniously taken in procession to the nearest open spaces and then interred, the chanting of hymns by the devotees reaching a crescendo. The *Bhaktas* hailed the Lord, taking His name, praying to Him to lead them on the right path, to make their Planet safe and secure against all attacks from across space.

The Raja was the patron of the *Utsav* at the capital. For ten days, the best of musicians and artists entertained the public at the huge grounds in the centre of the city. The best of classical musicians regaled the audience with their divine voices or their mastery over musical instruments; the most popular of dancers whirled on the stage to the beats of the music presented by the accompanying artistes, capturing the subtle nuances of *bhava* and reflecting the *navarasas.* Puppeteers and magicians and circus artistes too found the festive time just right for displaying their skill and earning fat fees.

On the last day, the big idol of the Lord was carried to the top of the highest mountain of the Planet, Olympus Mons, which puffed out smoke eternally. Then, amidst beating of the cymbals and music of the bands, the idol was dropped down the huge mouth of the volcano to merge with the fire that emerged from deep within, while the ardent devotees went into ecstasy. The final rites marked the end of the festive season. The Lord, everyone believed, had gone back to the hottest regions that lay at the core of the planet, keeping watch over the Planet and securing its safety through a network of fiery angels whose very presence lit up the setting and made the Planet look RED to any distant observer.

The astronomers on the Earth, who had been studying the Planet for thousands of years, noticed the red tinge and gave Mars the name, *The Red Planet*. They sought scientific explanation for the phenomena that would be consistent with reason and logic. But the Martians, at least the vast majority of them, believed that the Planet's top shade owed its all to fiery angels, on duty round the clock, keeping vigil from their observation posts atop the four tall mountains of the Planet.

Legends spoke of the feats and deeds of the Lord who destroyed evil and protected *dharma*. Each temple for the Lord had its own *sthalapurana,* the story behind the evolution of the temple. The Lord, they believed, reincarnated on Mars to defend the good and to demolish all evil. The

Marsehwaraleelotsav celebrated the victory of good over evil. Priests chanted the thousand names of the Lord. Scholars narrated the tales of the Lord, quoted from the *Masrveda*, the holy work that detailed the highest values set before the people to guide them through life and take them closer to salvation. The two major Epics, the *Marsayanam* and the *Mahamarsaratha* projected the multitude of facets of greatness of the Lord and His consorts and cohorts.

The Epics asserted that the horn on the right side of the Lord was the Sun.

Initially the people believed that their Planet was at the centre of the Universe and that the Sun and the rest of the planets revolved around the Lord. Since the Lord stayed on Mars, they assumed that the Sun and other planets and stars owed everything to their Lord. They asserted that every object they saw in the sky was going round and round, paying homage to their Lord. Very much like devotees who circled the *prakarams* of the temples, propitiating the Lord.

This Marscentric Theory held sway for millions of years. "That doesn't seem quite right," said Super Marsian, a scientist, who lived about a million Earth Years (EY) ago. (The Martian Year is approximately double the normal year of 365 days that we know). His statement whipped up passions on a scale, never before witnessed. He was condemned as a heretic, sniped at for disturbing the established order of things, jailed and told to recant.

The fracas was forgotten soon. But the truth he had espied refused to go away. Super Marsian had sown the seeds of doubt and triggered the curiosity of subsequent generations of scientists. His grand theory refused to die. It took thousands of EYs more for the truth about our Universe to find acceptance. The facts the scientists presented were so forceful that none could nail down the conclusion that Mars went round the Sun as a lie. Reluctantly, at first, and then, without much ado, people conceded that Mars and other Planets had elliptical trajectories with the Sun as one of the two foci.

Identifying the Sun as Marseshwara's horn helped the Martians not a little bit to regain their pride. This was one assumption the Martians clung to tenaciously. This belief became cardinal to their very existence.

But raging debates were still on about the second horn of the Lord. There were two schools of thought.

One set of people had no doubts about the association of the second horn of the Lord with Phobos, the bigger and nearer of the two moons of Mars. Not more than 16 EK (Earth Kilometre) in diameter, staying at an average distance of about 6000 EK, Phobos went round the planet, once every eight Earth Hours (EH). Young lovers saw in Phobos a passionate and ardent partner of the Sun, who could not be away from the Sun, who resided in the horn of Marseshwara, for more than eight hours at a stretch. Those who held Phobos in great esteem argued that it was the most zealous mistress of the Sun and remained always at the beck and call of her Lord and master. Martian women were told to be like Phobos. By identifying the second horn of Marseshwara as the symbol of Phobos, they wanted to establish its primacy.

They sneered at the other moon of Mars, Deimos, half in size in comparison to Phobos, whirling around at a distance of about 20,000 EK from the Planet, for staying so far away from the Sun. "It knows its insignificance. It keeps its distance," said the storytellers, adding, "Once Deimos played truant and earned the wrath of the Sun. In anger, the Sun sent her into exile in the wilderness of space, where she continues to whirl around, ignored and humiliated and left out in the cold. She hopes that some day, the Sun would forgive her and take her back into his fold. That hope sustains Deimos. But we see no redemption for her. Not after what she did to the Sun."

The legends spoke of how the Lord got his two moons. He had seized them and made them his own while they floated through space and came in to take a closer look at him, the God of Mars, also known as the Lord of War. (Later the Earthlings, who called themselves Romans, too, accepted Mars as the God of War).

This theory held sway for long. Then science came up with the right explanation.

Scientists found out that the Earth's Moon was a chunk of the Earth itself. The piece had been forcibly ripped out and thrown into space when the Earth dared to raise its eyes defiantly at a heavenly body that came close to its orbit. The Martians believed that this heavenly body was Mars itself. The chunk of Earth was hurled out into space with such tremendous force that it flew up quite some distance and, when gravity finally reduced its speed, it settled into an orbit round the earth and became a moon of the earth.

Not so the moons of Mars. They were actually asteroids that had strayed off course and got close to the gravitation belt of Mars. They were captured and then forced to go round and round Mars, for all times to come.

Science however did not completely erase the legend that associated the horns of the nation's God with the Sun and the satellite of Mars, Deimos.

The second group refused to believe that the horns of Marseshwara had anything to do with the Sun and the two moons of Mars. But they too were not free from the superstitious belief that the two horns were the source of strength of the Lord. In their eyes, the horns were the visible signs of all knowledge and wisdom. "The Lord's brain cells are in the horns. One set of brains is located in the horn on the right; and a reserve set in the other horn. We Martians, therefore are doubly blessed. Those dimwits on the Earth have just one set of brains."

Modern scientists thought the beliefs absurd.

But even they conceded that they owed much to the horns. The horns made the Martians invisible to those who did not have the horns. This became apparent every time someone had a mishap and his horns got damaged; or one got caught in squabbles or melees and ended up losing the horns. The loss of horns brought in its wake loss of the ability to see other Martians. It was assumed that the unlucky ones who had been deprived of the horns had lost their sight. But their eyes were perfectly normal. That baffled the medical researchers. After years of study, the scientists realized that the horns held a special gene. This gene was a sort of key that made it impossible for those without the horns to see those with the horns. That discovery boosted the pride of the Martians. They felt totally secure because if ever the Earthlings launched a massive assault on Mars, a danger that always nagged the Martians and was looked upon as a distinct possibility, they would remain invisible and thus take the enemy by surprise. That knowledge made the horns more precious in the eyes of the Martians.

Many doctors started horn implantation clinics to help those who lost the horns in one mishap or the other. A number of industrial houses churned out products to strengthen the horn or special shields to secure its safety during conflicts or quarrels. In the eyes of the Martian Law, willfully depriving a fellow Martian of the horns was considered as serious a crime as murder and the suspect, if found guilty, received the death penalty.

In the horns, the Martians espied the roots of their power. Belief in the horns, whether based on age-old myths or modern scientific facts and its special gene, breathed confidence into the whole race. The horns were prime to the existence of the Martians. Their pride and confidence were rooted in these beliefs. They assumed that the Earthlings would never equal them when it came to civilisation and intelligence and skill. That gave the logic behind the design of the Planet's flag that carried the horns, sharply etched in green, in the background of red. The Planet's anthem too praised Lord Marseshwara and hailed the powers of the horns.

The Martians had no doubts that they owed all that they considered valuable . . . their life, their progress, their advancement . . . to the horns. The horns were their strength, their Guardian Angels.

The majority of Martians were confident that no harm would come to them, since their Lord and the fiery angels were ever around to protect them and to defend them. However Raja Marspati and his advisers, both political and scientific, did not leave everything to God. They kept a close watch on every source from where the Planet could face danger. The Earth headed the list of possible source of danger.

For millions of years, Mars held technological superiority. Only in the last five hundred Earth Years or so had the Earthlings made rapid progress in the field of science and technology.

The agents of Mars, posted on the Earth, filed regular notes on the quick pace of technical advancement on the Earth. They also gave insights into the psychology of the Earthlings. Mars, the Earthlings knew, is the Planet's nearest neighbour. One weakness of every Earthling related to jealousy of one's neighbour. The Earthlings admitted that the high lifestyle of the Jones next door often turned one green with envy. Often they confessed that one can't live with one's neighbours nor can one live without them. Mars and the Martians, therefore, were always suspects in the eyes of the Earthlings.

How could the Martians make the Earthlings realize that the Martians meant them no harm? Nobody knew. Not even Raja Marspati.

The mood of Raja Marspati, on New Year 2004 on the neighbouring Planet, the Earth, was anything but cheerful. Disturbing news had been coming from the officials of the Departments of Planetary Intelligence and Security and also the Ministry of Defence, assigned the task of securing the safety of the Planet, that the slimy two-legged creatures of Planet Earth had sent out a few space ships to gather information about Mars. He was also alerted that some of the space ships might try to land on Mars to carry out ground surveillance and reconnaissance and also to find out if life forms existed on Mars. The report added that two Rovers, Rover Spirit and Rover Opportunity, were programmed to land on Mars and search for forms of life that need not necessarily be akin to those found on the Earth in structure and composition and evolution. That, certainly, was disturbing news.

The Raja was reaching out for the horn to steady his feelings when Vidyaswami, the Marspradhanmantri, a wizened old figure with a slight paunch and thinning hair that made his horns stand out, prominently, walked in. He bowed to the Raja and waited.

"Come with me," the Raja led the way, walked to a set of cushioned sofa on one side of the veranda, occupied one of them and invited the Marspradhanmantri to be seated.

"Are the intelligence reports we now have of the plans of the Earthlings to land Rovers on Mars true, my dear Vidyaji?" the Raja lifted his eyes and focused them on the minister.

"It is true, Maharaj, that the Earthlings are making all efforts to unravel the secret of our dear Planet. This is nothing new. This has been going on since the day man developed the ability to think by himself.

"Mars was an enigma to the Earthlings, for long. For an observer of the Earth, as we know, Mars moves sometimes forward and at other times retrograde, across the sky. That confused them for millions of years. They saw the red face of Mars and thought our Planet was the God of Wars. They too believed, as we once did, that the Sun and the other Planets went round the Earth. In 1609 of the Earth Calendar, two sky watchers Johannes Keplar and Tycho Brahe made observations with the naked eye . . . ,"

"Can the eye be naked," the Raja joked.

"Barely possible, Maharaj," Vidyaswami chuckled, remembering that BARE and NAKED were synonyms, before resuming his narration, "The two astronomers worked out the laws of motion of Planets, something we knew a million years before man," a touch of pride added a glint to his eyes.

"Keplar," he continued, "discovered that Mars orbited the Sun in an elliptical path. He added that the motion was non-uniform, but predictable. Fifty years later, another astronomer of the Earth, Huygens tracked down dark areas on Mars and referred to them as Syrtis Major. In the year 1666 of the Earth Calendar, Gian D. Cassini discovered our Polar icecaps. He concluded, correctly as we know, that Mars takes 24 Earth hours 40 Earth minutes to go round its axis. William

Herschel was the first Earth astronomer to talk about the seasons of Mars. It was only in Earth Year 1877 that the Earthlings got to know of our two Moons. Since then they have developed very powerful telescopes to study our Planet. But they still do not know much about our Planet. They hope to find out through space probes. Now they have the technological skill to do that," Vidyaswami paused.

"I agree. That became apparent in Earth Year 1969 when two men landed on the Earth's Moon," Raja Marspati remembered.

"Now the Earthlings are getting ready to pry into Mars and Venus and Jupiter and other Planets of the Solar System and also worlds beyond the Solar System. Mars is now a high priority area of study for the Earth scientists. They have shaken free of the belief of Giovanni Schiaparelli and Percival Howell that Mars has a network of canals made by intelligent beings to survive by utilizing the waters of the polar ice caps on

Mars that was turning inhospitable for life. In 1965, U.S. spacecraft Mariner 4 flew past Mars, took photographs and then the theory of the canals ended."

"You are a walking encyclopedia of almost every branch of knowledge," Raja Marspati complimented him.

"If I were not that, would you have chosen me to be your chief adviser, Maharaj?" Vidyaswami's lips sported a smile.

"Vidyaji, don't the Earthlings know that our Planet is a twin of the Earth? Take, for example, the time our Planet takes to go round its axis, once. It is about 24 Earth Hours 40 Earth Minutes. Just 40 Earth Minutes more than the time it takes the Earth to go round its axis once. Like the Earth, our Planet goes round the Sun, in an elliptical orbit," Raja Marspati felt a slight itch on the tip of his nose, chose to rub the itch off with a scratch, and joked, "There is always a scratch for every itch."

"And a twitch of the nose for every sneeze that waits to have its say," Vidyaswami laughed and his potbelly quivered like the string of a bow, plucked by strong hands. "You were comparing the Earth with our own dear Planet, Maharaj. Half the Earth receives the sunlight, always. So it is with Mars. The Earth takes 365 Earth days to go round the Sun. Our Planet takes nearly double that time. To be precise, it takes 687 Earth days for one *parikrama* of the Sun."

"We are farther from the Sun," the Raja quipped.

"That is true, Maharaj. The average distance of our Planet from the sun is 226,600,000 Earth km. So the orbit of our Planet is much longer than the one the Earth traces. That is why our Planet takes longer to go round the Sun. The distance from the Sun also affects our climate. The temperature at the Equator of Mars at noon in summer doesn't exceed 21 degree C. At night it goes down to – 80 degree C. The references, Maharaj, are also by the standards set by the people of the Earth," Vidyaswami took a break.

"When did we accept the standards set by the Earth? Why didn't we develop our own standards?" Raja Marspati cupped his chin with the palm of his right hand.

"We have our standards. But a commission, set up about 100 years back, found that the decimal system on use on the Earth is much more viable for making quick calculations. You know that we have Martian agents, all over the Earth. A force of five hundred, spread all over the Earth. They are everywhere, in the icy Polar region of the Earth and also in the hottest regions mostly around the equator. They are in almost every major capital city of the Earth. They are our eyes and ears. They have access to all that is happening on the Earth. They play their hands deftly to make the denizens of the Earth fight among themselves. Such internecine fights leave the people on the Earth little time to make a concerted bid to explore and to find out more about our Planet. Mars, they themselves admit, is a Superior Planet. This Superiority comes from the fact that our Planet is placed farther away from the Sun than the Earth and hence has a trajectory that is much longer than that of the Earth. Our Planet is the brightest object in the sky to an observer on the Earth. Our agents say that the scientists on the Earth assume that there is no life on Mars. Can anything be more absurd?" Vidyaji let a smile touch his lips.

"Let the Earthlings live with that belief, continue to be ignorant morons in their self-created Fool's Paradise," Raja Marspati laughed.

"I think they are determined to crack the shell of ignorance. Part of their ignorance, Maharaj, has its roots in our skill to camouflage the presence of life on Mars," Vidyaswami chuckled.

"One chuckle deserves another," Raja Marspati too chuckled.

"The Earthlings are proud of themselves. They claim that they are God's finest creations. Yet they have their fears. Their fears powered a very popular novel by H.G. Wells, an English novelist of great repute. He talked of Mars attacking the Earth. Years later, in the Earth Year 1938, Orson Welles recreated the novel on the electronic media. He started with the warning that it was just a story, being presented. But he made it so realistic that those who tuned in, after the warning was sounded, thought it real. They got the fright of their lives. The roads, leading away from New York, to the suburbs and the towns far beyond, got cluttered within minutes with vehicles, carrying people whose only goal was to get to safety before the Martians attacked them. Never had New York seen such frenzy. The report was a farce, just a hoax, yet it roused the darkest fears of the Earthlings."

"Scared by a farce!" Raja Marspati laughed.

"And that too of us, when we have, for ages been practicing peace," Vidyaswami chuckled.

The two took time to free themselves from the chuckles.

Then the blazing light of a flying object caught their eyes. They hurried to the far end of the Veranda, tracing the path of the object that seemed to descend and come down to settle into the dusty plains of the Planet.

"What is that?" Raja Marspati clasped his hands, intertwined the fingers and swung the mailed fist as if challenging the unknown object. A million furrows formed on his forehead, reflecting the thoughts that ran through his head.

Vidyaswami didn't reply. Instead he picked up the field glass that he had brought along and focused on the object. The Raja followed suit. They stood, watching the object with total fascination.

The Earth Calendar showed the date as January 4, 2004.

The flying object was Rover Spirit. It did not burn out on entering the Martian atmosphere, thanks to the heat shield. The retro rockets slowed down its speed of descent. The parachutes opened up without a hitch. A cushion of balloons made the landing safe. In six minutes, Rover Spirit touched down on Mars, at Gustev Crater, just South of the Martian Equator.

The strange sight of the landing of the probe vehicle, sent by the Earthlings, electrified the mood of Raja Marspati and also Vidyaswami. They knew its name too. It was Rover Spirit.

"That is the latest machine sent by the Earthlings to pry into our secrets. This is the fourth of such object to land on our Planet," Raja Marspati's eyes gained a steely glint.

"And if the reports filed by our men on the Earth are right, we could expect another such machine, called Rover Opportunity. It is expected to land, in about a fortnight, at a point diametrically opposite to the one where the object has landed." Vidyswami replied.

"I hope the strategy we have devised works," Raja Marspati had his fears.

"It will, Maharaj. We have already gone through all that, a dozen times, if I remember right. We have made contingency plans to knock out the vehicles that land on Mars, whenever we decide to do that," Vidyaswami's voice quaked, slightly.

"I sometimes wonder whether it would be better to destroy the intruding machines as soon as they enter our atmosphere," the Raja pouted his lips.

"We have the technology needed to pulverize the object at the time of our choice. We can intercept it while it gets close to Mars by just sending a beam of fiery Marslaser that turns to ashes the hardest of shells, spun with the finest of steel. We even have the Mahamarsastra, the powerful Ray that can turn the Earth into ashes if we focus the beam on the Earth for a few seconds. But we decided to take a close look at these machines sent out to our planet. We wanted to know more about them. We shall keep the Rovers under constant watch. We shall blow them up if we sense even the slightest sign of danger. Or, we shall cripple them with minor mechanical intervention and make them as helpless as a turtle turned on its back. Our scientists have the right strategy to handle the Rovers. So there is no room for panic," Vidyaswami assured the Raja.

"I know, I know, but suppose the Rovers bring with them some bacteria from the Earth? Suppose the strange bacterial form of life is let loose on our Planet? Have we the means to contain the danger?" Raja Marspati fixed a glance on Vidyaswami.

"I think no bacteria from the Earth can survive on our planet."

"Are you sure? I am told that bacteria can survive in the coldest of cold areas, as much as in the hottest of regions that are simmering cauldrons," Raja Marspati had his doubts.

"How can anyone be absolutely certain, Maharaj? Certainty is for the Gods. Only Lord Marseshwara knows for certain. But I think the structure of life on our Planet is so different to that on the Earth that the alien bacteria will die within seconds of arrival here. That is what I have been told by the head of our Genetic Research Centre, Dr. Marsvigyani. I believe him. He is the best of genetic scientist on our Planet. I am sure he is right."

"If he is not?"

"Should we cross the bridge before we come to it, Maharaj?"

"No. But we must be ready to take the bridge, if the need arises. We must have plans for every contingency."

"We have them, Maharaj. Rover Spirit is under close watch."

"The Earthlings want to track down life on Mars."

"Rover Spirit has a special equipment to do that," Vidyaswami nodded his head.

"And if it manages to confirm our existence?"

"Maharaj," Vidyaswami's voice rose by a decibel or two. "We had agreed that we would let the Earthlings find out about life on Mars. That was why we let Rover Spirit land. Otherwise we could have shot it down when it descended. Remember how we incapacitated the earlier space ship Beagle 2, sent out by . . ." Vidyaswami could not get the word, *Europeans*, right till Raja Marspati came to his help. "The Europeans."

"Are they telling everyone that they are `U ROW PEONS'? I mean peons who occupy lowly ranks and find places for themselves somewhere at the back, where one usually finds ROW U?" Vidyaswami punned.

"You have a way with words, Vidyaswami, but this is not the time for puns. A misplaced pun never holds any fun," Raja Marspati's voice was curt and stern.

"Sorry, Maharaj! Our agents in European capitals say that the scientists who sent Beagle 2 were hoping against hope that the space ship would manage to land on Mars safe, that it would snoop around and gather information about us. Because we heard of its arrival in advance, we could intercept it in time and demobilize it. It now has found its last resting place in the dusty surface of our Planet. That confirmed we have the power to destroy the intruding vehicles whenever we want."

"You said it."

"We decided two days back, when we knew Rover Spirit would land today, to use the occasion to explore other possibilities, of establishing contacts with the Earthlings. We know what Rover Spirit and Rover Opportunity carry. They have SSTR that can sense and see life forms on Mars and also read our minds. We shall test how effective the SSTR is. I can ask our men to disable Rover Spirit temporarily to make the Earthlings realize that they can't take the end result for granted," Vidyaswami rolled on.

"I know. But I sometimes I get a feeling that this may lead to new complications," Raja Marspati had his fears.

"We have worked out all the alternatives. No harm will come to us. That much is certain," Vidyaswami paused before adding, "May be, this will open up new opportunities, Maharaj. May be, we are about to create planetary history.

"That sounds quite a thrilling possibility," Raja Marspati pepped up his spirits and got ready to be at the centre of all action that he expected the landing of Rover Spirit and of Rover Opportunity to trigger.

"That is it, Maharaj. I have posted a team of observers and strengthened the defence arrangements around Gustav Crater and also around Meridiani Planum, the flattest smoothest region of Mars, half way around the Planet from the spot where Rover Spirit landed, where we expect Rover Opportunity to land, a fortnight hence," Vidyaswami's eyes gazed across space to take a fresh look at Rover Spirit that squirmed around, on its Lander, slowly balancing itself on its six wheels so that it could roll off the Lander and start Operation Mars.

❑❑❑

3

The Swing of Spirits

A yawn is no respecter of persons. It does not spare anyone. It chooses its victim from every strata of society. The King can't deny the yawn the right to have its say; nor can a pauper ward off a yawn when it chooses him for exercising its democratic right.

Dr. Cockroff, having spent 24 sleepless hours, watching the landing of Rover Spirit on Mars and its state of operational efficiency, could not check the yawn on January 4, 2004.

His mouth opened wide, the array of teeth got exposed while the chin dropped down and the upper lip arched and a gush of air rushed out, defining it as one of the most evocative of yawns of recent times.

He had watched Rover Spirit bounce up and down a dozen times before coming to rest on the surface of Planet Mars. His fear of a last minute complication had been proved to be false. One fear died. But there were an array of new fears that held him in their hold. One fear put out was not enough to restore to him his mental poise.

The knock on the door was the last thing he wished for. Yet the knocks were insistent.

"To hell with the caller!" he cursed under his breath, before adding, "Come in."

The pounding continued.

"Didn't I say, Come in?" he shouted.

"I can't. The door is locked," said the voice of Dr. Sastri.

"Oh, my God. I forgot," Dr. Cockroff rose groggily from his seat, slid out through the narrow edge between his rotating chair and the ornate table, walked up to the door and turned the knob that held the door in a locked position.

"Thought I should congratulate you, personally, on the successful landing of Rover Spirit," Dr. Sastri too looked a little bedraggled, but his posture reflected the fact that he was brimming with joy.

"Too early to gloat over the landing, my friend. Do you know that I am just a bundle of fears?" Dr. Cockroff moved across to the coffeemaker and set the controls in motion.

Dr. Sastri hung around, his long nose sniffing the air, before adding, "Nothing like a hot cup of coffee when it comes to smothering fears!"

"You like coffee with milk and sugar, while I like black coffee," Dr. Cockroff started gathering the hot brew in a beaker.

"Strange, isn't it, that you who drink black coffee is fair-skinned, while I who love coffee with milk is brown-skinned" Dr. Sastri joked.

"Here is your coffee," Dr. Cockroff gathered the decoction and milk and sugar in a mug, stirred the mix with a spoon and handed over to Dr. Sastri. He prepared a mug of black coffee for himself.

The two sat side by side on a sofa, set against one wall of the big room, in silence for a minute or two to get their spirits revived by the coffee.

"You should not be a bundle of fears, now that Rover Spirit has landed on Mars, Cocky. Does not COCKY indicate excessive ego and self-confidence? So live up to your name," Dr. Sastri broke the silence, playing with the senior's name.

"It is not that simple as all that, Param," Dr. Cockroff let out a deep sigh. "The energy supply of the Rover may get snapped. Can we discount the possibility of failure of some sensitive equipment? Mind you, there are too many of them on board the Rover. That thought gives me the creeps," Dr. Cockroff realized that he was sitting with a stoop and sat bolt up right, before adding, "My friend. It is too early to count our chicks. They have not hatched. Not as yet."

"One of the eggs has hatched. Rover has landed safe," Dr. Sastri sounded optimistic.

"One swallow doesn't make a summer," Dr. Cockroff refused to push his fears out.

"Why can't you be an optimist?" Dr. Sastri growled.

"Because I see things misti-optically," a sly smile lit up Dr. Cockroff's lips.

"That sounds better," Dr. Sastri emptied the last dreg of the coffee and rose to make another cup for himself.

Dr. Cockroff watched him, his eyes narrowing, wondering what made Dr. Sastri tick. He had come half way round the globe, found his feet in the world of scientific research, yet clung to the vestiges of his days in India. Dr. Cockroff didn't get the right word though Dr. Sastri often referred to his days in India as his *poorvashram*. He claimed he was a Saivite, one who worshipped Lord Shiva. Yet he was equally devoted to the Lord of Tirumalai, Lord Venkatachalapati, who had a tongue twister of a name for anyone, much more so for a God of the *Vaishnavites*.

Dr. Sastri saw no contradiction in this dual faith. "I know that Shiva and Vishnu are one and the same. They are manifestations of God. So they could as well be Ishwar, Allah, Christ. You name any God; and you find that you have taken one of the names of the ONE GOD to whom we all owe our everything," he had told Dr. Cockroff once when he teased him for riding two religious sects in one go.

"Kipling must see you," Dr. Cockroff drank the last bit of coffee in the mug and set it on the table. "He would then have realized that the East and the West have met in you."

Dr. Sastri settled down with the second cup of coffee, offering no more than a wry smile to his senior's comment.

"Why are you tongue-tied?" Dr. Cockroff nudged him.

"Have you ever seen a tied-up tongue?" Dr. Sastri growled, before adding, "I am gathering my wits."

"So even wits can be gathered?"

"If brains can be picked, why can't wits be gathered?" Dr. Sastri snapped in good humour.

"Why can't you make the East and the West fuse?"

"Into what?"

"A baby," Dr. Cockroff looked at Dr. Sastri with a glint.

"The SSTR is my baby. In it you find the *Gyandrishti* or extra sensory perception of the Orient; and the technical skill of the Occident. So . . . ," Dr. Sastri held his face at an angle, letting the light cast the shadow of his nose prominently on the wall.

"The shadow of your nose has landed safely on the wall." Dr. Cockroff quipped.

"Don't mistake the shadow for the substance or you will miss every opportunity that comes your way to make good," Dr. Sastri countered.

"Who cares? All that matters to me, now, is the smooth continuance of the activities of Rover Spirit and the safe landing of Rover Opportunity," Dr. Cockroff brought the focus back on what was of immediate concern to them.

"It still has nearly three weeks of travel before its gets close to landing on Mars. So, the formula of not trying to cross a bridge till we come to it keeps me cool," Dr. Sastri said.

"You and your sense of detachment!" Dr. Cockroff hit the ceiling with a sharp comment.

"I live this moment. Worry is tomorrow's mouse, eating today's bread. I can't let that happen, so Lord Vekata . . ."

"Save your breath. Param. You don't have to take that long name. And, then, is it fair to disturb God by taking his name so often? Didn't you tell me that the Lord answers every call we make to Him?" Dr. Cockroff pouted his lips.

The conversation gamboled, with the ease with which mountain goats skip and romp around, covering a wide variety of topics, not all of them confined to science or more specifically to the Mars Mission. The session continued till Dr. Sastri noticed the yawn that Dr. Cockroff failed to hold back and rose to leave.

"Thank God! Rover Spirit is not a living thing. Only living things get tired and seek rest. Machines can work on and on and on. Forever if only the energy they need is provided continuously. Rover Spirit's energy pack has been well stacked. Solar energy too will power the Rover. So I hope it starts moving, gathering all the information we seek and transmit the photographs and the data that shall help us know more about Mars," Dr. Cockroff yawned once again.

Dr. Sastri wished him a good night's sleep and left.

Dr. Cockroff's eyelids were heavy. His eyes were bloodshot, weary, tired. He tried to resist the call of sleep, but he dropped off. How long he slept, he did not know. But when he woke up, after the long slumber, he was once again brimming with energy.

All his waking hours, he spent tracking the progress of Rover Spirit on Mars and also of Rover Opportunity getting close to Mars. He felt elated when Rover Spirit took slow but steady steps, started studying the area around. He felt now confident that Rover

Opportunity too would land on Mars, at Meridiani Planum, the chosen point, almost half way around Mars from Gustav Crater.

It was January 15, 2004, EY.

Dr. Cockroff switched on the machine that matched the SSTR on board Rover Spirit. The sight that greeted him made his eyes pop out. He saw armed figures, with horns, taking position at some distance from the area of activity of Rover Spirit. The figures marched in perfect order. The scene reminded Dr. Cockroff of the impeccable turn out by young officer cadets at their passing out parade.

The printer attached to the counterpart of the SSTR on board Rover Spirit stirred into action. It printed out the message from Rover Spirit. (The Rover referred to itself as I. Dr. Sastri and his team had programmed it to speak in the first person singular).

A group of weird figures are heading to where I am now. They have horns

on their heads. They are riding a strange vehicle that looks akin to a battle tank. It glides very fast over the loose red soil.

The men are holding small gun-shaped objects. I sense they are some special type of laser guns.

The group is now getting closer.

I can read their thoughts.

Ah! They don't mean to blow me up. They are thinking of putting me to sleep for some time. They want to test if they could do what they like with me. They want to immobilize me, temporarily. They want to incapacitate my equipment, for a short period. So I face no immediate danger, though for some time I won't be communicating with you.

Of course, they will not hesitate to blow me up if they sense danger. That much is certain.

Ah! A dart is rushing toward me. It hits me on the side. Is it a sedative for almost human machines like me? I think so. Oh, I am feeling sleepy. So sleepy that I feel like just snapping all the wires and the gadgets that make me work and going off into a long slumber.

Ah! Forgot to tell you. Those who are putting me to sleep know of the SSTR.

That took Dr. Cockroff by surprise. Had he read right? Or was he giving wings to his fears and seeing illusions? He rubbed his eyes vigorously, before reading the report again. He slumped into the sofa and sat like one mummified, his mind working feverishly to examine the report and to decide if there was any truth in the statement of Rover Spirit that it sighted intelligent life forms on Mars and that the aliens knew of the SSTR. The possibility seemed very remote. It sounded like a yarn spun by one of world's best liars.

Then he dismissed that thought. Rover Spirit was a machine, programmed to report facts. Humans could tell lies, indulge in prevarications and even churn out fanciful tales that would sound so realistic that the listeners might be fooled. But that was the last thing one expected of Rover Spirit.

"That makes the exercise quite interesting, though I can't for the life of me guess what twists and turns the Mars Mission will take now," Dr. Cockroff spoke to himself, keeping his voice low.

His thoughts meandered.

The intelligent life forms on Mars, he surmised, had the ability to put Rover Spirit out of action, at will. They had demonstrated that. For there was no more response by the counterpart of the SSTR on board the Rover located at Ground Station. The printer too had gone off into a state of indolence, the bright red light indicating that its electrical circuit, however, was in fine mettle. The printer, Dr. Cockroff told himself, would print only when there was an input from the other end. It was keeping a vigil, like a solitary guard atop a watchtower, waiting for signals to come from the field of action. That was all that the printer could do. It was only a medium, just a messenger. It could report nothing on its own. That power belonged to Rover Spirit.

Alas! The Rover had been drugged and put out of action, temporarily. Or so said Rover Spirit before it sank into hibernation. And there was nothing that anyone on the Ground Station could do to spur the Rover quickly into action. Or could something be done?

An idea came to Dr. Cockroff. He could instruct those who had prepared the circuitry to clean up the instructions of the computer on board Rover Spirit that had been affected by the sedative shot and send in fresh instructions to reactivate it.

He was toying with this idea when he saw the door swing on its hinges. Who dared to walk in without even a knock? His eyes zeroed in almost instantly on Dr. Sastri, whose normally bright eyes looked pale and listless. He did not hail Dr. Cockroff with his usual cockiness. Instead he quietly came over, slid into a chair and sat with his chin, cupped in his palms, peering at Dr. Cockroff.

"What has come over you, Param? You look pale and beaten. Have you seen a ghost?" Dr. Cockroff growled.

"Ghost? I don't believe in ghastly ghosts. They are figments of imagination. Only the scared and the cowardly believe in ghosts. You know I don't belong to that group," Dr. Sastri firmly rebutted the statement, before adding, "Ghosts are not for real. But I now know for a fact that there is intelligent life form on Mars. I also am pretty sure that the Martians have been keeping us under watch, for long. How stupid of us to assume that we are probing for life on Mars, while the Martians have been very much in our midst, gathering every bit of information about all our activities, including every mission to Mars, organized by us. Remember Viking 1 that went into an orbit round Mars on June 19, 1976. The lander touched down on Mars at the golden plain Chryse on Mars on July 20, 1976?"

"I also recollect the landing of Viking 2 at a picturesque site, 7400 km away from where Viking I touched down on Mars, a couple of months later. We named the site Utopia. Going further back, I recollect Mariner 3's successful flight getting as close as 10,000 km of Mars and sending back 21 photographs of the Red Planet before streaking off into the vast expanse of space. Mariner 6 went still closer. We finally managed to put Mariner 9 into orbit on 13 November 1971. It remained in contact with us for about an year."

"Mariners always serve well. They are hard and tough and survive the vagaries of long journeys, even in the vast ocean of space," Dr. Sastri cut in before adding, "Are you going to dwell on Mars 1 and Mars 2 and . . . also of how some of them succeeded and others failed . . ."

"Failures are stepping stones to success, Param," Dr. Cockroff perked up.

"An old faded proverb," Dr. Sastri snapped.

"Every proverb is decocted wisdom of ages," Dr. Cockroff countered, sharply. Then he remembered that they were going round in circles when both needed to examine the available facts that indicated that intelligent life forms existed on Mars.

"Well, Dr. Param. Do you know that Rover Spirit has been drugged and is no longer operational?"

"My God! Does that mark yet another failure in our quest to unravel the secrets of Mars?" Dr. Sastri fixed Dr. Cockroff with a firm glance.

"Oh no! On second thoughts, I think we have struck pay dirt."

"Does anyone pay for dirt?" Dr. Sastri played with the words.

"I mean, we now know for certain that Martians are for real. They have immobilised Rover Spirit."

"I have independent proof that Martians have been keeping us under watch for ages."

"I am all ears," Dr. Cockroff sighed.

"When it comes to ears, the donkey gets pride of place," Dr. Sastri joked.

"When will you learn to be serious?" Dr. Cockroff struck a disapproving note.

"When we stop sparring," Dr. Sastri suppressed a chuckle and resumed his narration, "I told you that Martians have been keeping us under watch. One of our scientists, engaged in finding out how effective the SSTR prototype is, was out testing the equipment to pick up different thoughts whirling around. After a long walk around the shopping mall, he decided to walk into a restaurant to recharge his energy."

"Man needs refueling from time to time," Dr. Cockroff joked.

"If that were not necessary, the zest for life would vanish, in a trice, and the world would turn into a drab place. There would be no exciting drama of survival, with the hunter developing new skills to catch its prey and dine on it to recharge its energy pack and the hunted discovering novel strategies and innovative tricks to escape the clutches of the enemy and to live for yet another day. It is this perennial battle for survival that provides the thrill of life. Would I ever have shaved off the tuft on my head, taken to the hairstyle of the West, shifted from *dhoti* and *angavastram* . . ."

"What is that? I find it hard to take the last word. It is yet another a real tongue twister of a word," Dr. Cockroff jibed, in humour, and laughed loudly.

"I will celebrate the occasion when I can feed you a word that not only twists your tongue, but ties it up in knots," Dr. Sastri joined the laughter, waited till the gentle banter's effect evaporated, and resumed, "The *angavastram* is a long loose clothe that can be shaped to suit one's mood. It can be neatly folded and thrown over one side of one's shoulder. Or it could be completely opened up and thrown with skill so that its middle section covers the back while the two ends hang around the shoulders, ready to be drawn tight across the chest or left to flap leaving enough space to reveal the hairy chest. It is an essential part of the traditional dress of the Indian male."

"It is his mail, if I may pun," Dr. Cockroff cut in. "You turned your back on the conventional style of your predecessors and came to the United States to . . ."

"Ensure that I have the finest of fuels to recharge my energy, from time to time," Dr. Sastri shrugged his shoulders, before shifting tack, refocusing the conversation on the experience of the scientist who had gone to the restaurant in the Mall to get some a quick bite and drink. "I was telling you about the field scientist . . ."

"We left him in the limbo," Dr. Cockroff smiled.

"We shall now restore him to centre stage. He got a plate of French fries, collected a huge conical glass filled with milkshake, flavoured with strawberry, piled over with chocolate chip ice cream, and sat down at one of the vacant tables. The SSTR hung round his shoulder by a long leather strap. After cleaning up the plate of French fries, he took a sip of the drink and felt a surge of energy. He turned the SSTR, which he had switched off, and moved it around idly while enjoying the drink. Then he heard a low whistle from the machine, indicating that it had sighted something. He stopped sucking out the contents of the glass and examined the screen of the SSTR. He noticed the image of a strange figure, shaped like one of the dwarfs that we see at the circus, with two stout but very short horns on the screen. When the scientist tried to pin down the figure, a waft of wind swished through and the figure vanished form the SSTR. However the thoughts that ran through the mind of the departing figure was registered by the SSTR. The scientist took a print out. I have brought it along for you to read," Dr. Sastri pulled out a folded sheet of paper from his coat pocket and held it out to Dr. Cockroff.

Dr. Cockroff's fingers closed in on the sheet. He carefully unfolded it and read the message.

> *My God! I, Marsspyringa, had a narrow escape. I think I got too close to the machine. I must be careful. Otherwise I will be caught and grilled and forced to give out the secrets that shall seriously damage the interests of my Planet Mars and of My Lord, Raja Marspati. I would rather die than fall into the hands of the Earthlings.*
>
> *If the SSTR is being used widely, the activities of agents of Mars, posted on the Earth to watch and report on the plans and activities of the Earthlings to learn more about Mars, will be*

severely hampered. We cannot move as freely as we could, till now, through the security areas.

I must report to Raja Marspati about the complication. He should know that the Earthlings have now developed the technical ability to carry out probes of Mars. They have space ships orbiting Mars. They have landed machines on Mars. I hope Raja Marspati has taken suitable action to check the movements of Rover Spirit and is also ready to collar Rover Opportunity that is expected to land on Mars on Jan 21, 04.

I shall send a telepathic message to Raja Marspati and alert him and also our Mahamantri ji and the chiefs of Defence and Intelligence of my Planet. So Marseshwara help me!

Dr. Cockroff's eyebrows arched up, indicating the state of his mind. He was not one who let excitement get the better of him, easily. But after reading the note, he could not restrain his feelings.

"So we were under watch. And we didn't suspect that this could be the case," Dr. Cockroff muttered under his breath, before reading the text once again, slowly, pondering over each sentence, eager to get not only the meaning of the text, but also to guess what possible import the news could have on the future course of events.

"We can be sure of one thing. There is intelligent life form on Mars."

"I already know that," Dr. Cockroff was brief in his response.

"You knew that? And, yet, you kept it a secret from me. Cocky," Dr. Sastri sounded put off by the news.

"I was about to tell you, but you didn't give me the chance. You had an exciting report to make; and I decided to give you the chance to have your say first. I think you should read the message I received from Rover Spirit before it was deactivated by none else but the intelligent beings on Mars. Read it yourself, Param," Dr. Cockroff nudged his colleague to seek out the SSTR.

Dr. Sastri read the message. It was incredible.

Two independent reports confirmed the presence of intelligent life forms on Mars.

Dr. Sastri also remembered a report from Sydney, Australia, that he read in a newspaper just two days back.

> *Australian scientists claim that a dog with a nose for sewage had found evidence that life once existed and may still exist on Mars. Biophysicist Tony Taylor said his mongrel had sniffed out a bacteria in mud from Queensland that match perfectly the fossils of primitive organisms in the Martian meteorite that plunged into the Antarctica 13,000 years ago and was retrieved in 1984. It is potato*

sized and called ALH 8400. Recent analysis confirmed life existed on Mars. Taylor had trained the dog Tamarind to sniff out sediments containing bacteria. "It smells like sewage and she knows the word STINKY," said Taylor.

"I think we are on to a trail hotter than those that the ace sleuth Sherlock Holmes ever chased," Dr. Sastri broke the silence that seemed pregnant with myriad possibilities. "We can now be pretty certain about life on Mars. And none can say that it is a cock and bull story."

"We are scientists and we go by proven facts," Dr. Cockroff drawled, when he remembered the last sentence of the message printed out by the counterpart of the SSTR and sprang from his seat.

"How stupid we can be! Rover Spirit has been put out of action and here we are, debating the presence of intelligent life forms on Mars instead of resurrecting the

Rover," Dr. Cockroff's lips quivered, while he fretted within.

"We aren't that stupid as you think, Cocky. We now know for sure that there are advanced life forms on Mars," Dr. Sastri cut in.

"Shall I call them Martians, concede that they are truly intelligent and have the ability to counter our moves, admit that Martians are members of a martial race?" Dr. Cockroff realized the validity of Dr. Sastri's comment and grinned, before adding, "We shall prove that we are more than a match for them."

"I am not all that sure, Cocky. It is time you shed your cockiness, accept the possibility that Martians are much more advanced than us. . . . ," Dr. Sastri suddenly got a brainwave. He bounced out of the seat, felt the numbness of the right foot and joked, "It is not Rover Spirit alone that has gone to sleep. Even my right foot has gone into a slumber," kicked the air around to restore the blood circulation to his foot and felt once again the firmness of the step he took.

"This is the Age of Sleep, be it for Spirit Rover or your foot," Dr. Cockroff joked, but Dr. Sastri was so taken up by the idea that he just managed to wave his hand and run out of the room like a man whose coattail was on fire.

Dr. Cockroff waited till the door shut, on its own, thanks to the springs and levers that operated the automatic door closure, before getting into action. He pressed the knob of the intercom to activate it and talked to a dozen people, ranging from head of the communication system to the computer specialist to the electrical circuitry controller to a host of others to tell them that Rover Spirit had got stuck and they must get together and take steps to spur the lazy Rover into a roving mood.

Operation Revival Spirit received top priority. The technicians checked but Rover Spirit refused to respond to commands from

Ground Station. The technicians and the scientists fiddled with knobs and switches and control panels and tangled loops of wires and transistors and plugs. All to no avail! Rover Spirit refused to be whipped back into operation. Yet the men at the Ground Station refused to accept that all was lost. They assumed that the Rover had only gone into hibernation and could be whipped back into shape.

Dr. Cockroff hovered around, moving from one room to the other, interacting with the personnel, offering them possible alternative courses to bring Rover Spirit back to life. But nothing worked. For more than a week, commands from the Ground Station streaked through space to spur it into action. It was feared that Rover Spirit might never roll on, exploring the terrain on Mars.

Yet the team at the ground Station did not lose hope. Rightly has it been said that hope remains eternal in the human heart.

Dr. Sastri rarely ever took part in this operation.

"What the hell is holding him back!" Dr. Cockroff groaned to himself.

He would have been thrilled if only he had even a vague hint of the hot trail that Dr. Sastri had picked up. He had noted that it required the SSTR to smoke out the alien. In other words, only SSTR could see the Martian. Not normal humans. For man the Martian was invisible. How could that be possible? How did the Martian manage to escape detection by the naked eye?

Then a string of thoughts ran through him. He went to the library to browse for hours through books on myriad unbelievable facts about life forms on the earth. He spent a major part of the night, searching for more facts through the Internet. Googles and Yahoos and other search engines were kept busy, hunting down facts that he needed to formulate his theory. Gradually the mist around the invisibility factor around life forms began to dispel. Dr. Sastri realized that invisibility was not impossible. He finally jotted down his conclusions in a note with the heading: *A Study in Invisibility of Shapes and Forms to the Naked Eye.*"

The brief summary of the paper read:

> *The SSTR, a machine that we fabricated to identify the presence and also to record the thoughts of intelligent life forms on Mars, when they are in the close vicinity of the machine, has sprung a surprise by spotting the shape of the Martian figure that remained invisible to our scientist, who held the machine, though he looked out for it.*
>
> *That holds one clear clue. The Martian has managed to make himself invisible.*
>
> *It took me some time to realize that invisibility goes with transparency. That may sound like a logical conundrum. Is not transparency the opposite of concealment? Yet it is by*

turning transparent that life forms become invisible.

Enough proof of this enigma can be seen on this earth. Yet we remain, by and large, unaware of this reality. I might have spent all my life in ignorance about this fact but for the SSTR.

How do we see objects? It is by the light it deflects. Thus, when we see something as red, we accept it as red in colour. We don't look into the reason. What really happens is that the object absorbs all the colours of the light but red. Suppose the structure of a life form is such that it doesn't deflect light, but lets light pass through its body?

That may seem impossible. Then we also remember that the impossible is more often than not a tag that goes with something inexplicable.

Are there life forms whose body structure makes the passage of light through them possible? My study of life forms on this earth reveals that the miracle does exist on this planet. Our Earth teems with life forms that we can't see through the normal eye. These life forms have made themselves translucent. That makes visual sighting almost impossible.

There are squids and fresh water shrimps that remain invisible when in water. The wings of some butterflies (Callitaera, for example) remain transparent and hence hard to see.

My study also led me to Mucopolysacharides and Collagens that work together to create transparency and thus translucence in life forms. I studied a few life forms. Then the basics struck me. These life forms have little or no blood vessels. There are no pigmentation cells. Further extra-cellular spaces are smaller than the wavelengths of light. The structural units are regular and repetitive.

Together they make the life form more translucent and hence hard to spot.

Suppose Martians have developed this technology to a state of perfection and genetically tinkered with their genes to make themselves invisible!

He sent a copy of the paper to Dr. Cockroff on January 28. Next day, he walked into Dr. Cockroff's room, after receiving a call from the former.

"That is indeed wonderful work, Param. You always come up with results far beyond my wildest imagination. I am turning green with envy, man, at your ability to find needles in haystacks," Dr. Cockroff drew Dr. Sastri in a warm hug.

"An object looks green when it draws all other colours in the spectrum unto itself.

May be, envy lends that power to man," Dr. Sastri joked.

"Green is for go, Param," Dr. Cockroff reached out for the intercom that buzzed loudly, cutting short the light banter, and identified himself, "Dr. Cockroff here."

"This is Bert Holt from the Rover Spirit computer repair team. I have good news for you, Dr. Cockroff. Rover Spirit has been revived, miraculously. It is true we wiped off the old instructions fed to the onboard computer. But we are not sure whether that was what worked the magic. At any rate, the Rover is ready to resume the task of investigating the composition of a rock named Adirondack left incomplete when it was put into a state of inaction."

"Thank you. I am thrilled to learn that Rover Spirit is back to work. That is the news that truly cheers. Why bother what brought about this result? Hope it doesn't run into problems again. Keep me posted of further developments, Bret," Dr. Cockroff ended the talk and shared the news with Dr. Sastri.

The intercom buzzed again. This time, the caller was Dr. Philiposis Pandolouse who headed the team constituted to study the photographs and reports to analyse the composition of the Martian soil. Dr. Philiposis clipped, with a slight Greek accent, "Dr. Cockroff, preliminary study tells us that the chemical composition of the soil is mainly of silicon and iron with small amounts of sulphur, chlorine and argon, a noble gas that is part of the Martian atmosphere. Also it contains considerable amount of Olivine that contains oxygen, iron and magnesium, usually found in volcanic ashes. One possibility is that the soil is simply ground up lava. The fine grains seem to stick together. Could be due to static electricity."

"Aha," Dr. Cockroff didn't seem to be terribly excited by the report. "Thanks for the news. I am waiting to hear when we go beyond the stage of guesswork with myriad possibilities and have conclusive evidence of the composition of the soil of Mars. I hope we won't have to wait for long. Good luck in your quest," Dr. Cockroff waited for the call to snap before resuming the conversation.

"Param, we know beyond a shadow of doubt, now, that Rover Spirit was put out of action by the Martians. That gives us a hint that the Martians are tech savvy. They are not morons, as science fiction presents them. That gives a new twist to our future course of action. How far advanced are the Martians? Are they ahead of us? If so would it do us any good to rub them on the wrong side?"

"So there is a right side and a wrong side, even to the Martians?" Dr. Sastri played with the idiom.

"This is no time to be flippant," Dr. Cockroff sounded deadpan serious.

"I didn't flip an ant," Dr. Sastri was never averse to a good pun.

"You and your accursed sense of humour!" Dr. Cockroff exploded, before sensing that he could unwind with a bout of laughter and piped in.

"ACCURSED is a combination of two words. It can be broken into AC, which is short for air-conditioned, and CURSED. So ACCURSED is something that is CURSED, yet enjoys AIR-CONDITIONED comfort," Dr. Sastri triggered more laughter with that deft definition.

"You should have gone the way of Ogden Nash or Oscar Wilde," Dr. Cockroff paid him a compliment.

"And NASA would never have got anywhere close to Mars," Dr. Sastri joked.

"What ego!" Dr. Cockroff scowled.

"Ego reflects self-confidence. One must have it in right measure to succeed in life," Dr. Sastri bantered.

"Now, Param, can we get back to the right strategy we should adopt toward the Martians? Should we keep nettling them with probes and thus earn their wrath? Or should we extend the hand of friendship to them? Perhaps if they too are eager to make friends with us, we could jointly explore the Galaxies and the worlds beyond. For Mars is a Superior Planet in this sense that it is farther from the Sun," Dr Cockroff shared a possible line of action.

"Would the Martians be interested in accepting our friendship? We have to be sure of that. Even if we get confirmation, the options you suggest are not ours to choose. That power vests with the President. We can only provide him all the facts. The decision is his to take. So, for the present, let us not step beyond the limits of our brief. Let us keep watch on Rover Spirit and . . . Ah! Rover Opportunity too has landed on Mars, exactly half way across Mars, on hard, rocky surface, at Meridiani Planum. Around here we expect to find Hematite that holds water. Is there water on Mars? Is it in extractable form? We must find out. I hope Rover Opportunity does that. Well, the Rover is about to step off the Lander. Ground Station is now busy adjusting the forward tilt of the Lander, pitching it down by 5 degree, to make it easy for the six-wheeled robot to get down on Martian soil. Let us check with the display counter that is directly linked to the SSTR on board Rover Opportunity, Cocky," Dr. Sastri suggested.

Dr. Cockroff nodded his head. He pressed a knob and the monitor blinked before projecting the image of a figure in royal finery, a crown deftly balanced on two short stout horns, watching Rover Opportunity in the company of a slightly older figure who too had two short stout horns over which stood an ornamental cap. Behind them stood a dozen others, all with horns on their heads, quietly watching Rover Opportunity.

The monitor flashed a message that made the hearts of both the space scientists miss a few beats.

❑❑❑

4

Spin in Harmony

The heart has its reasons when it skips a few beats. Just a few beats when it gets terribly excited or scared. Once the limits of safety of missed beats is reached, the heart frees itself from the state of rest and gets back into the rhythm it must maintain to sustain life.

The hearts of both Dr. Cockroff and Dr. Sastri did just that.

The screen projected the group of Martians and also continuously presented the heated discussions among them. Thought waves identified the figure with the crown as Raja Marspati, the ruler of the Planet, and the slightly older figure by his side as the Prime Minister of the Planet, Vidyaswami.

"No society ever thrives without power centres. We are turning our backs on royalty, but Martians have their Raja," Dr. Sastri shared a random thought that came to him.

"Don't assume that just because the feudal system of royalty exists on Mars, the Martians are backward," Dr. Cockroff reacted.

"Who knows who is backward and who is forward? Don't you know that Einstein was considered backward while at school? Yet . . . ," Dr. Sastri didn't say anything more because he knew he had made his point.

"Let us move forward with what is of immediate concern to us, Param," Dr. Cockroff's voice quivered, slightly, indicating the emotional pitch of the thoughts within.

Dr. Sastri nodded his head.

The two focused on the SSTR Monitor to read the continuous stream of thoughts of the Martians that streaked across the screen. The essence of the thoughts that streamed was recorded by Dr. Sastri, very good at preparing briefs that cut off all flap, yet never missed any of the salient facts.

His brief ran like this.

1. *The Martians claim that they had successfully 'killed' the European Mars probe, Beagle 2, which landed on Mars on Dec 12, 2003, EY, in order to make us understand their capability to defend their Planet. Tacit in the fate that befell Beagle 2 is the message that nothing lands on Mars unless the Martians let them land.*

2. *The Martians let Rover Spirit land on January 4, 2004, to see how and where it differed from Beagle*

2. *Having completed the study, they debated what to do with Rover Spirit. Finally it was decided to knock it out, for a few days and to have fun watching the panic reaction of the Earthlings. That too was done with ease. The Martians used a powerful weapon to send Rover Spirit into hibernation.*

3. *They revived it to prove to themselves that they had the capability to keep an intruding vehicle in a state of animated suspense for periods of their choice. The results had been absolutely satisfactory. Martians believe they could blow out an alien machine; or freeze it for long periods. In other words, they could play the cat and mouse game, making the intruding ships from the Earth the mice for their games.*

4. *The Martians are keeping Rover Opportunity under watch. They have decided to let the Rover conduct the experiments we have in mind. They see no immediate danger to their Planet from the Rovers. So they have decided to let the Rovers continue their studies.*

5. *What is of much more immediate interest to us are the observations about the evolutionary story of the Martians. The conversation between Raja Marspati and his chief adviser Vidyaswami indicates that billions of years ago, much before civilization began on the Earth, Mars was like our Planet. The air had enough Oxygen to sustain life. Water too was available in abundance. In those days, the average Martian looked like any man on the Earth, today. He gained a high level of intelligence. He discovered the*

secrets of nature, adopted many of the tricks of nature to improve the life style of the Martian. He burned immense amount of fossil fuels to meet the energy needs of the populace.

6. *The ecologists and the environmentalists of Mars warned of the danger latent in the uncontrolled misuse of the Planet's resources. They threw up their hands in dismay when their warnings about the adverse impact of mounting pollution failed to make an impact on the powers that be. The Martians who held power continued their quest for progress with zest. They ignored the resultant environmental degradation and increasing pollution and change in the climatic conditions. The warming up of the Planet created serious problems. The Ozone*

layer developed holes. The level of Oxygen in the air began to dip drastically. The quantum of Carbon dioxide in the air increased by leaps and bounds. The ecologists cried themselves hoarse, dwelling on the dismal future, but their cries fell on deaf ears. "We have the answer to every situation," said the scientists involved in developmental projects. "We are confident of finding an answer to climate change by deft use of genetic engineering."

7. *Fertile land became infertile. Ground water level dipped sharply. Low-lying areas were inundated. Life could no longer be sustained in the form in which it existed.*

   The scientists took on the task of using technology skillfully to ensure survival. They tinkered with the genes to gain the ability to breathe in Carbon dioxide and process it so that the Oxygen sustained life while the carbon, subtly handled in a sort of incinerator, embedded in the body, developed with the help of gene technology, provided the energy the body needs.

They altered the structure of the body, made it transparent so that the sun's rays just passed through the body and didn't permeate to heat up the body. That minimized the demand of the body for water. They developed technology to munch ice cubes to quench their thirst.

Because the body is transparent, the Martian is almost invisible. The scientists restructured the shape of the body of the Martian. They added, with genetic tinkering, two short stout horns. The horns hold the genes that enable the Martian to see other Martians.

8. *It seems, when such changes were happening on Mars, some Martians, totally dismayed by what they dubbed as the madness of their brethren, keen to retain their close links with nature, eager to retain the human form that seemed to them perfect in every way, left the Planet in space ships and landed on the Earth and populated the Earth.*

9. *The Martians believe that the humans who now populate the Earth are the descendants of the deserters who took to flight in space and turned their backs on their native Planet. So, they share something in common with the Earthlings.*

10. *They are now seriously considering various options. One of the options that Raja Marspati discussed with his advisers revolves around cementing friendship between the*

people of the two Planets. Then the best of brains of both the Planets could join hands and work together to understand the secrets of other planets of the solar system and also of the Milky Way and the Galaxies that stretch unto infinity in space. He is instructing the chief of the group of Martians, who have been spying on us and whom we caught on the SSTR recently, though we failed to seize him, to find out whether the Earthlings are in a mood to make friends with Martians. If his report is positive, Raja Marspati hopes to hold talks with the ruler of the nation that successfully sent the Mariners and the Rovers and to work together to explore the Universe.

Dr. Sastri read the brief, checked it for accuracy, made a few corrections and passed it on to Dr. Cockroff, while asking, "What do we do with it now?"

Dr. Cockroff read it, carefully. He read it not once but three times. Then he put it on the side table and turned to Dr. Sastri, a slightly puzzled look in his eyes.

"How much can we rely on the SSTR?" he asked after a minute's silence.

"My faith in it is beyond doubt, Cocky," Dr. Sastri replied.

"I, whom you call Cocky, is haunted by doubts, while you, Param, is cocky about the results of the study made with the help of SSTR," Dr. Cockroff still could not shake free of his fears.

"The coward dies a thousand times," Dr. Sastri gently reminded him.

"Caution is the key to survival. So you can't blame me if I exercise caution," Dr Cockroff justified his stand.

"The man who can acts. Others wait and wait, ignore the knocks of opportunity and later rue their mistakes," Dr. Sastri cut in.

"What should I do?" Dr. Cockroff was caught on the horns of a dilemma.

Dr. Sastri felt sorry for the man. He knew the root of the problem faced by Dr. Cockroff. He would be held responsible if the report, prepared on the basis of the feedback by the SSTR, turned out to be deliberate false information, fed in by the Martians. Yet, he saw no harm in keeping the doors open for negotiations while continuing the study.

For quite some time, the two remained lost in their thoughts. Finally Dr. Cockroff rose, saying, "My mind is foggy. May be a cup of hot coffee may clear the fog."

"How about fetching me too a cup of coffee? Coffee with milk and sugar! Not the black variant that you prefer," Dr. Sastri grinned.

"Why do you need a drink? Not even a whiff of doubt clouds your understanding of the situation," Dr. Cockroff pouted his lips.

"I need the drink to strengthen my conviction that my understanding is right," Dr. Sastri smiled.

"I wish I have equal faith in the SSTR," sighed Dr. Cockroff, while turning the knobs of the coffee maker, after placing the beaker under the nozzle of the machine, waiting for the hot beverage to flow into it.

"You see facts in black and white. I see it in the colour of brown. Can I say that the complexion of the skin gives the distinct angle of vision?" Dr. Sastri joked.

"You have a joke for every occasion. Often the jokes are at your expense, yet you don't blanch. That is what I like about you, Param. You can laugh at yourself," Dr. Cockroff patted him.

"No junior dares to laugh at his senior. That is the golden rule of survival in the hierarchical system of every organization," Dr. Sastri took a jibe at the senior.

The two enjoyed the cups of coffee, while discussing the report in depth. Finally the two agreed to forward the report to the President of the United States through the official channel. For the issue involved policy decisions that could be taken only by the political leadership.

*****

George Bush, the President of the United States, was on board the special aircraft taking him for a weekend holiday with his wife. The cushioned seat sucked him into it, while he leaned back, stretched his legs and threw his arms at the back of his head and felt totally relaxed. All play and no work, the proverb says, make Jack a dull boy. It lifted his spirits when he saw the proverb from a new angle and told himself, "All work and no play make Jack a dull man."

Turning dull was the last thing he wanted to happen to him. He had worked his schedule skillfully, finding time to relax

NASA
NASA

in the midst of all the problems that landed on his desk. He knew he held the most powerful office in the world. It would prove disastrous to the whole world community if he stumbled or fumbled due to mental or physical exhaustion.

Every President, without exception, kept fit through some form of exercise or the other. Even the polio-stricken FD Roosevelt, who had to take to the wheelchair to move around, kept himself fit by swimming. The President's immediate predecessor, President Clinton, found in the daily run through the footpaths that encircled the White House, located at Washington DC, the right means of buying himself good health. The normal traffic was not held back or diverted while the President kept pumping his legs with the energy needed to keep a steady pace. A couple of security personnel kept behind him discreetly, checking the scene to ensure that no harm came the way of the nation's Chief.

President Bush had himself been a fitness buff, all his life, and rarely missed a chance to have a daily run. And, whenever he could, he flew out of the capital, spent time playing golf with his friends, cruised on the blue waters of the sea, recharged his energy and returned, tan, but not wan, ready to resume the onerous duties that devolved on him. From morning till late at night, he was at work. Often, it was well past midnight that he retired to bed.

Many Presidents had admitted that they must have been mad when they decided to make a bid for the high office. Yet this was one madness that powerful people . . . senators and governors from both the principal political parties of the land, and, once in a way, even retired officials of the Services, festooned with ribbons and medals and reputations of their successful campaigns in defending the interests of the country, on battle fields, mostly beyond the borders, against rulers out to weaken the nation's supremacy. . . willingly opted for.

The aircraft cruised, at a steady speed, at a height of about 4500 meters, yet for those on board, the aircraft seemed to be hung in space, perfectly at rest, letting them relax fully.

The President had learnt to push the problems of the office he held out of his mind, when he left on holidays. Yet he did not succeed in freeing himself on all occasions from the problems of his office. There were times when he felt weighed down by some serious problems. He had faced it during the days following the tragedy of 9/11 (Short for September 11). On that day, three years back, terrorists crashed two Aircraft on the world Trade Centre at New York. The towering structure crumbled like a house of cards. That had made him go after Osama bin Laden, alleged to be the brain behind the dastardly act. The President ordered army action to clear Afghanistan, of the terrorists and to reclaim the land for democracy. Then had come the suspicion of Weapons of Mass destruction (WMDs) in Iraq and the military action that ended with the collapse of the regime of President Saddam Hussein and establishment of American authority in Iraq.

On this flight, the President did not feel fully relaxed. A vague indefinable anxiety cast its shadow on his peace. This anxiety had its roots in the report of Dr. Cockroff which he had read, an hour before he left on the holiday. He had held hurried consultations with the Secretary of State and also the Secretary of Defence.

How much could he rely on the conclusions drawn from the study conducted with the help of the SSTR? None could say, for certain. He had read the report thrice. He knew all the points raised by Dr. Cockroff.

Could it be possible that Martians were technologically more advanced than man? If that was indeed true, could man ever afford to antagonize the Martians? They could well be in possession of more powerful weapons of defence and offence than what humans held.

He let his mind recollect the salient points of the report of Dr. Cockroff. He recollected that they had been together at School. Even in those days, Cocky, as everyone referred to him, was focused. He had no time for the rumble and the tumble of student life. For him science, specially Physics, held all the pleasures he needed. George Bush then was a fun loving young man, from a rich family, who found no academic subject so captivating as to cast a spell on him.

In those days, Cockroff viewed George as a charming young man who drew friends unto him like a magnet attracting iron files. He sensed that some day George would be a leader of men. That had come true, though it was, if one may say so, by a cat's whisker that he managed to wrench the right to occupy the White House from Al Gore, the Democratic Party's candidate.

Cockroff was proud of the fact that his old schoolmate now led the most powerful

nation. George, in turn, kept track of the role of Cockroff in keeping America in the lead in the field of Space Research. Yet but for exchange of New Year greetings, there was hardly any contact between the two of them. Each moved in a different orbit till the report brought to the President the need to discuss the matter in detail with the scientists. For the time had come for deciding on the future course of action in the relation of the Earthlings with the Martians.

"Let me talk to him," the President let the words escape his lips.

"To whom?" the First Lady asked.

"Dr. Cockroff, my dear. He heads our Mission to Mars."

"Haven't you enough on your hands with problems on this Earth?" her voice had an edge.

"The future of the Earth cannot be seen in isolation. The Earth is part of the Solar System. And the Solar System is only a speck in the vast expanse of the cosmos," the President gently pressed her hand, noticed her face gaining a glow of happiness and quickly asked the communication officer on board the aircraft to connect him to Dr. Cockroff over the hotline.

"Good morning, Mr. President," Dr. Cockroff greeted the President as soon as he came on the line, taking just a fraction of a second to decide not to address him as Bushy.

"Morning, Dr. Cockroff. I have just read your report. It sounds fantastic. Can we rely on it, absolutely?" the President too chose to be formal.

"Mr. President, is there anything absolute on this earth?" Dr. Cockroff drawled.

"How much credibility can we give to this conclusion that the Martians are keen to befriend us?"

"Mr. President, I would look at it from a different angle. Have we anything to lose by exploring the possibility of friendship with the Martians? If the Martians truly desire friendship, we have to hold talks with them. Of course, we have to exercise caution, Mr. President. At the same time, in my humble opinion, we have to dare and act. We should not rue, later, that when a golden opportunity came our way, we just failed to pick it up. Pardon me for taking the liberty of speaking out my mind so freely . . ." Dr. Cockroff paused.

"That's what I like about you, Dr. Cockroff. You don't mince words."

"Thank you, Mr. President."

"Give me a day's time"

"To munch over the issue, Mr. President?" Dr. Cockroff joked. "Or shall I say, Bushy, reverting to first name basis we enjoyed till you became the First Citizen of the country."

"I have always looked upon you as Cocky."

"Don't be fooled by the image, Mr. President. Deep within, I am a bundle of nerves."

"Who is not? A deft mix of caution and daring is what we exercise all through life. I don't want to enter any terrain that angels fear to tread. Yet, I can dare and act because the Martians are not angels. They too are mere mortals in this sense that they have not escaped death," the President paused.

"Death is the end of life, for sure. But how much one can achieve during a lifetime? So let us celebrate life, Mr. President," Dr. Cockroff maintained the formal mode of address though he almost felt a desire to use the name BUSHY and continued, "I've taken too much of your time. The issue is off my hands."

"I am now the baby sitter."

"The buck stops with you, if one can go by the words of former President Harry Truman."

"I may not see eye to eye with late Mr. Truman on many issues, but he hit the nail on the head when he identified the location where the buck stops. Well, in case we decide to pick up a dialogue with the ruler of Mars . . ."

"His name is Raja Marspati."

"Well, in case we opt for talks, are you sure you can establish the necessary link up and also the means to make intelligible conversation?"

"Leave that to me, Mr. President. The SSTR can be fine-tuned to keep the dialogue going by empowering the parties to go beyond mere words and read the thoughts," Dr. Cockroff explained.

"That makes it hard for us, politicians, who are good at what is known as double speak. Often we say what we don't mean," the President had a dig at his tribe.

"It is time, Mr. President, that politicians learn to be transparent," Dr. Cockroff quipped.

"You are forcing it on us," the President joked.

"You won't regret it, Mr. President. The age of spinning yarns and fooling the people has to end. Why can't you be the man to bring about that change?"

"You can be very persuasive.

"Thank you."

"Well, you are sure we can read the minds of the Martians?

"As much as they can read yours, once we gift an SSTR to them. Or, perhaps they have already copied our design and need no gift."

"Suppose we deny them the gift. Suppose they haven't succeeded in the effort to duplicate the SSTR?"

"Then there can be no talks. For SSTR alone can interpret thoughts and make them meaningful. If the Martians don't have it, they won't ever know what we want to convey to them. SSTR is a double-edged weapon. It takes no sides. It plays fair and square. It stays neutral. It is not like the Frankenstein monster that turned against its creator."

"So, if the Martians are up to some mischief, we will know that for sure."

"Right, Mr. President."

"Thank you for that assurance. I shall get back to you soon, Cocky. Bye," the President paused and added, as an afterthought, "Best wishes, Cocky. Bushy wishes you all the best," and the line got snapped.

Dr. Cockroff gaped at the ceiling, while his thoughts hovered around the immense possibilities that friendship with Mars would open up.

It was not often that the President used the private line to call Kofi Annan, the Secretary-General of the United Nations.

The President, after reviewing the salient features of the talks with Dr. Cockroff, decided that he would have to take the world leaders into confidence. For though he had his pride in the fact that he was the unquestioned leader of the world community, he still knew the limits beyond which even the President of the United States could not impose his authority on public opinion in all parts of the globe. America was not a colonial power that held all other nations in a state of bondage. Material power lent to the voice of America the magic power to have its way, on most occasions. Dangling the right bait in the shape of monetary aid worked wonders when it came to bringing even the most critical of world leaders into more pliable moods. If the lollypops failed to work the magic, the President could turn to threats and blandishments, though even he had to cloak the dangerous moves behind a veil of high moral principles. This was so every time the nation took to arms to have its way, be it in Afghanistan or in Iraq.

But, on this occasion, the issue that the President had to handle concerned all mankind. It involved the future of the Earth and its relationship with Mars. He did not want to take a unilateral decision and force it down on all mankind. He knew that world leaders, be they to the Right or to the Left or placed somewhere in between, claiming to be Non-Aligned, would agree to sink their differences and gear up to handle the sensitive issue. For it was not a tug of war between nations of the world. The future of mankind was at stake. Nobody knew for certain the military power of Mars. So a wrong step might mark the end of man. That thought gave the President of the United States the jitters. He sensed the need for collective wisdom of mankind in handling this explosive issue. The one man who could make this possible was Kofi Annan.

Kofi Annan was standing before a mirror and straightening his tie when the telephone rang. He let the tie hang, with a loop double the size of his neck, deciding to tighten it round the neck after attending to the call. He picked up the receiver and identified himself.

"Morning, Mr. Secretary-General. This is George Bush."

"Morning, Mr. President."

"I want a special session of the UN General Assembly."

"I thought the need for such sessions ended after your unilateral action in Iraq," Kofi Anna's voice indicated how hard it was for him to forget the fact that he was forced into playing the role of a spectator when the United States and Britain joined hands to have their way in Iraq. He almost added, "Or have you found Weapons of Mass Destruction in Iran?" but killed the words before they spilled out. He did not want to relive the bitterness of the days when the United Nations watched helplessly the tragedy enacted in Iraq. The future mattered. None was more aware of that than Kofi Annan.

"Mr. Secretary-General. I beseech you, call a special session to discuss and debate our future course of action on the current space probe of Mars. We have come upon certain facts that need to be debated at length by the leaders of all nations. One wrong step could mark the end of man. That is no exaggeration," the President averred.

"I trust your judgment, Mr. President," Kofi Annan chipped in.

"Are you not curious to know more about the situation? Specially when it could mean life or death for man?" the President felt that the Secretary-General was cool, didn't show much warmth though he maintained formal courtesy.

"I am listening," the Secretary-General still seemed rather tepid.

The President decided he would get down to business. He was confident that once the Secretary-General got all the facts, he would hasten to call the special session of the United Nations. So he raced through the latest news on the space probe of Mars. He shared with the Secretary-General all the details he now possessed. Kofi Annan's lower lip dropped when he heard that intelligent life forms had been spotted on Mars. It seemed incredible when he learnt that the Martians were technically very advanced. They had put Rover Spirit in a state of hibernation and later revived it. Impossible, it seemed to him, when he was told that the scientists at NASA had developed a machine that could see invisible forms and also read their thoughts.

Kofi Annan did not interrupt the President till he had all the facts. Then he broke the silence and asked, with some trepidation, "Are you certain, Mr. President, that you have got all the facts right?"

"I can vouch for them, my dear Sir. For my information comes from quarters most reliable," the President sounded sure of himself.

"I shall call a special meeting, Mr. President, of the United Nations. Please send a formal request," Mr. Kofi Annan suggested.

"It is on its way, Mr. Secretary-General. The load is off my head."

"I am now carrying the baby," Kofi Annan laughed.

"You are the best man for the job."

"I understand, Mr. President. Leaders of all nations dump their problems on my lap and expect me to babysit them," he laughed.

"I like to hear you laugh, Mr. Secretary-General."

"How I wish I could laugh more often! But, no, you world leaders won't let me have hearty laughs. Yet I sometimes manage to have a laugh, even though it is often dry and wry."

"Cheer up, Mr. Secretary-General. Life can't be all that bad for the most powerful civil servant of the world."

"And so can't afford to be uncivil," Kofi Annan laughed, this time more loudly.

"Thank me. I gave you a chance to laugh," the President shifted tack and said in a somber tone, "Thank you, Mr. Secretary-General. I now await the special meet of the United Nations. Bye, till then."

Kofi Annan set the receiver back and reached out for the two ends of the tie. He pulled the ends till the knot of the tie moved up and snugly slipped into the slot between the two flaps of the collar

The next few days were historic.

The media, both print and electronic, reported the details of the special session of the United Nations, convened to discuss the right policy that man should adopt to avert danger from inter-planetary conflicts. The members of the United Nations authorized the President of the United States to seek the hands of friendship, on behalf of all mankind, with the ruler of Mars. He was told to take the world leaders into confidence of all developments, on a day-to-day basis. The broad lines of the approach strategy too were defined.

Raja Marspati was pacing restlessly across the sandy terrain when Vidyaswami walked in. He bowed, politely and waited for the nod.

"Come, Sir. I need your help, now, more than ever before," the Raja took a deep breath.

"I am at your service, Maharaj. Always at your service."

"I know. How glad am I that I have in you a trusted and tested adviser!" the Raja grinned.

"I am your humble servant, Maharaj. At your command, always."

"Tell me, oh Noble Sir, can we trust the Earthlings? Remember, they are the offspring of deserters. There is another name for deserters. Rats. You know it, don't you?" Raja Marspati looked at Vidyaswami.

"I know, Maharaj. We have to be cautious. At the same time we have to push ahead our agenda. For a million years, we have been hoping to explore the Milky Way and also pry into the secrets of the world beyond. We are better placed than the Earthlings because we are not that close to the Sun as the Earth is."

"But when we compare the vast expanse of space, the distance between the Earth and our Planet seems to be very small. So small that it looks a dot in the stretch of space. Miniscule is the word that comes to my mind," Raja Marspati's finger slid over the horn for a fraction of a second.

"Everything is relative, Maharaj. Even distances," said Vidyaswami.

"We knew about Relativity a million years ago. The Earthlings found out about Gravity only five hundred EY s back. And it was only a hundred EY s back that they came to know about Relativity. We are better equipped to handle relative issues. So we can lead the discussions. The Earthlings will fall in line, easily."

"I have my fears, Maharaj. These Earthlings are no fools. Take, for example, the SSTR. We never imagined the need for such a tool. The Earthlings have stolen a march over us in thought reading, I think."

"Give the devils their due," the Maharaja conceded.

"Those whom we like are angels. All others are devils. May I add that one group's devil is another group's angel?"

"That is a truly witty parody of an old cliché. Yet there is much wisdom latent in it. You owe your all to your brains. You are the finest think tank on Mars," the Raja patted Vidyaswami on the shoulder, thus confirming how much he valued the old man's advice.

"Shall we ask the head of our group, keeping watch over the activities at the NASA station, to procure us an SSTR? Or can we develop one indigenously?"

"We have already done that, Maharaj."

"You have?"

"Yes. When we put Rover Spirit to sleep for about a fortnight of Earth Time, we dismantled it, piece by piece. We took a close look at the high-resolution panoramic cameras, mounted on a vertical telescopic arm. The cameras are programmed to take photographs that will help the men at Ground Station in Earth to choose which soils and rocks to analyse and where to guide the robot once it is in motion. We took a close look at the antenna that facilitates transmission of data directly to the Earth. We examined the on-board computer system and also the complex machines and robots and technical support systems. None of them, however, is more advanced that what we have developed. In fact, most of them are primitive, says our Scientific Adviser. It is the SSTR, however, that is novel and new. Our technical team is now fabricating a prototype. I expect it to be ready in a day or two."

"That quickly?" Raja Marspati found it hard to believe.

The two heard someone rushing in. They turned and noticed the Scientific Adviser Marsvigyansadhak hurrying toward them. He bowed to the Raja, then to Vidyaswami and waited for the Raja's nod.

"I know you have news for us," the Raja smiled.

"Yes, Maharaj. We have prepared the prototype of the SSTR. It works well. We tried to read the thoughts of a few Martians with the help of the machine. Now we know how often people lie. This machine is the best thing that could have happened to us. Its presence is enough to make one speak the truth. For, even if he remains silent, we know what he is thinking," the scientist sounded proud of himself and his team.

The SSTR helped communication between the President of the United States and the Supremo of Mars. The talks were frank and free because thoughts, not words, helped the talks. And neither knew how to twist and turn around thoughts to gain undue advantage.

Later, Dr. Sastri who monitored the talks, held through the SSTRs, prepared a brief.

On February 17, 2004 EY, the President of the United States held Thought Exchange with Raja Marspati, the Ruler of Mars, with the help of the SSTR.

Raja Marspati spoke of the old ties between Man and the Martian. He stressed the fact that millions of years ago, Mars was like the Earth. And the Martians, then, were like humans. They didn't have horns. They needed Oxygen to survive. All that changed when the Martians burnt indiscriminately fossil fuels. They cleared forests, felled trees and developed chemicals like fluro-carbons and pesticides and polluted the Planet. They went through the same stage of development in which man finds himself today. He traced

> *the history of the DESERTERS who took a spaceship to populate the Earth, then uninhabited by intelligent beings. "We condemned them then. Now we know that they were right. You, Mr. President, and all humans are distant cousins of the Martians," he said.*

He advised the President to take all steps immediately to save the Earth. Otherwise the Earth would turn inhospitable. And then Man would have to genetically grow horns, breathe Carbon dioxide and draw out Oxygen and also energy, live on a planet that would sport no trees, no sea or lake or pool. The weather pattern would undergo immense change. Slowly the Planet would turn into a twin of Mars.

"Now is the time to save the Earth from that tragedy," said the Raja. He pointed out that the Martians had gained immense technical advancement. "We had to find ways and means to survive after Mars

turned virtually into a huge poison pack. We did that. Genetic engineers worked out the changes needed by the Martian to survive in this changed settings. Engineers found means of transportation over sandy soil and rocky terrain, developed aircraft that could fly even when wild winds raced across the Planet. We too are driven by a desire to know more about our Universe. The Martians knew space travel a million years ago. You have developed that skill only recently. But you have developed advanced technology of which we have no idea. We admire the invention of the SSTR that has made our talks possible today. Let us join hands to probe the Milky Way and the Galaxies and find out more about the origin of the Universe.

The President, on his part, expressed happiness. "Blood, Maharaj, is thicker than water. It cheers me to know that we are cousins. Thank you for warning us of the future that awaits us if we don't save the Earth from pollution. I shall take all possible steps to fight pollution. We can also help

you, Maharaj, to reclaim the Martian soil. We have developed the technology to reclaim vast sandy areas for cultivation. We shall send you saplings that shall withstand the weather conditions of Mars and put in roots and cover Mars with huge forests in course of time. The weather pattern will change. A day may come when you won't need horns any longer to survive. The future is ours to be. Together we shall make the future rosy," the President remarked.

"I have only heard of roses. Never seen them," Raja Marspati groaned.

"You will see them soon," the President assured.

Rover Rosy was the name of the next mission to Mars. It had on board three potted rose plants. Raja Marspati was present at the site of the landing of the Rover. Its descent was slowed down by eight de-orbit rocket engines. A heat shield protected the Rover from the heat caused by friction when it entered the Martian atmosphere. When the descent speed dropped down to about 1000 km/h, a parachute took over. The Rover hovered around at a height of 1,000 metre when the parachute was discarded. A series of lander rocket engines slowed it down further. When it touched down, it was moving at a speed of just about 8 km/h. The Rover settled down on Martian Soil. A hatch door opened. A mechanical arm pushed itself out, carefully balancing a steel plate on which rested three potted rose plants, sporting huge red and white and yellow roses. The plate also had an ornate card, with the message: *With love from the Earthlings to the Martians. May our friendship grow from strength to strength! May the twins spin hand in hand in harmony for all times to come!*

❑❑❑

References

1. Mission to the Planets by Patrick Moore:
Cassell 1995.

2. Exploring the Planets: Mars by Duncan Brewer: *Cherrytree Books 1992.*

3. Stars and Planets by Patricia Lauber: Collins *1967.*
Several articles/ news reports in newspapers/ Magazines during Jan/ Feb 2004 when US Rover Spirit and Rover Opportunity landed on Mars.